Artificial Intelligence And LegalTech Essentials

Advanced Series On Artificial Intelligence (AI) And Law

Dr. Lance B. Eliot, MBA, PhD

Disclaimer: This book is presented solely for educational and entertainment purposes. The author and publisher are not offering it as legal, accounting, or other professional services advice. The author and publisher make no representations or warranties of any kind and assume no liabilities of any kind with respect to the accuracy or completeness of the contents and specifically disclaim any implied warranties of merchantability or fitness of use for a particular purpose. Neither the author nor the publisher shall be held liable or responsible to any person or entity with respect to any loss or incidental or consequential damages caused, or alleged to have been caused, directly or indirectly, by the information or programs contained herein. Every company is different and the advice and strategies contained herein may not be suitable for your situation.

ISBN: 978-1-73-460163-3

DEDICATION

To my incredible daughter, Lauren, and my incredible son, Michael.

Forest fortuna adiuvat (from the Latin; good fortune favors the brave).

CONTENTS

Note: Visuals are collected together in Appendix B, rather than being interjected into the chapter contents, for ease of reading flow and to see the visuals altogether.

Dr. Lance B. Eliot

ACKNOWLEDGMENTS

I have been the beneficiary of advice and counsel by many friends, colleagues, family, investors, and many others. I want to thank everyone that has aided me throughout my career. I write from the heart and the head, having experienced first-hand what it means to have others around you that support you during the good times and the tough times.

To Warren Bennis, one of my doctoral advisors and ultimately a colleague, I offer my deepest thanks and appreciation, especially for his calm and insightful wisdom and support.

To Mark Stevens and his generous efforts toward funding and supporting the USC Stevens Center for Innovation.

To Peter Drucker, William Wang, Aaron Levie, Peter Kim, Jon Kraft, Cindy Crawford, Jenny Ming, Steve Milligan, Chis Underwood, Frank Gehry, Buzz Aldrin, Steve Forbes, Bill Thompson, Dave Dillon, Alan Fuerstman, Larry Ellison, Jim Sinegal, John Sperling, Mark Stevenson, Anand Nallathambi, Thomas Barrack, Jr., and many other innovators and leaders that I have met and gained mightily from doing so.

Thanks to Ed Trainor, Kevin Anderson, James Hickey, Wendell Jones, Ken Harris, DuWayne Peterson, Mike Brown, Jim Thornton, Abhi Beniwal, Al Biland, John Nomura, Eliot Weinman, John Desmond, and many others for their unwavering support during my career.

And most of all thanks as always to Lauren and Michael, for their ongoing support and for having seen me writing and heard much of this material during the many months involved in writing it. To their patience and willingness to listen.

CHAPTER 1
AI AND LAW

CHAPTER 1
AI AND LAW

CHAPTER 1

AI AND LAW

Artificial Intelligence (AI) and the field of law, a great conjoining of two fields, sharing equally with each other in a bidirectional manner and producing a unique intersection that finds itself rapidly growing and attracting immense attention.

Interest in AI and the law can be traced back to the early days of the AI field -- the first International Conference on AI and the Law was held in 1987, serving as a kind of cornerstone or hallmark for this field of inquiry.

There seems to be an innate and ongoing quest to find ways to apply AI to the law.

Most recently, given the latest advances made in AI technologies, there is a palpable resurgence of interest in AI and the law, including that investors have recently plunked down over one billion dollars ($1,000,000,000) in AI and law-related startups, based on high expectations of explosive growth in this arena (per indications by the National Venture Capital Association or NVCA).

Maybe we'll finally make some truly substantive progress and go beyond the earlier simplified versions of AI and the law.

One aspect that many decry is the dearth of real-world applications that are a genuine and deep intertwining of AI and of law.

Allow me a moment to elaborate.

Many lament that AI and the law hasn't seemed to grab sizable traction and has been bumping along for quite a while.

An often-expressed qualm about why AI hasn't done more with the law field is that trying to find experts that know AI and also know the field of law is seemingly as scarce as hen's teeth.

You can either find a law researcher or law practitioner that knows something scant about AI, or you can find AI experts that know only a smattering about the law, but it is precious few that seem fully versed in both domains at the same time.

It is my sincerest hope that this book will serve as an impetus to further bring together those in AI and those in the field of law.

In fact, welcome to those of you from either discipline!

That being said, let's clarify that the combination of AI and the law can mean different things to different people.

We need to straighten out that confusion straightaway.

The Two Subfields Of AI And Law

For ease of articulation, I usually depict AI and the law as consisting of two primary areas of focus:

- AI as applied to the law
- Law as applied to AI

They are both crucial.

Neither one is somehow more important or more invigorating than the other. They each have their place.

What is the difference between them?

In the use case of AI as applied to the law, this generally means that you use AI to participate in the performance of legal services.

To make sure we are on the same wavelength, please know that AI is a type of technology (which will be explained herein) and not some magical creation.

Today's world has seen a rapid rush to apply technology of all kinds to nearly every field of endeavor.

Indeed, there is a mania these days with tagging the word "Tech" onto the end of various domains, such as FinTech for financial systems technologies, MedTech for medical systems technologies, and so on, and the field of law gets its own tag too.

Specifically, today you refer to any tech as applied to the law as either **LegalTech** or **LawTech**.

In the next chapter, I'll explain how those two new keywords are being used and what they specifically encompass.

Returning to the matter at-hand, one way to think about AI and the law consists of considering how to exploit a myriad of AI techniques and AI technologies for the enactment and application of the law.

That's AI as <u>applied to</u> the law.

Roll out the red carpet for the **Robo-Lawyers**.

I cringe to say this, but some do refer to AI as applied to law as so-called robo-lawyers or robot lawyers, which I loathe and bring up to merely offer that the catchy phrasing does conjure a vivid imagery of what is meant by AI as applied to the law, though don't let the imagery overtake your sensibility.

Please do know that we are far afield of any kind of walking and talking robot that could act as a lawyer, thus, you can put down your pitchforks and rest assured that we aren't there as yet.

That being said, keep those pitchforks handy since someday we might achieve that kind of capability.

Another common expression pertaining to AI as applied to law involves referring to the emergence of the **Super Lawyer**.

One interpretation is that a Super Lawyer is a human lawyer that is aided by AI, thus becoming a human lawyer with "super" powers (the AI augments their human normalcy with super capabilities).

Another version of Super Lawyer is that AI will be so powerful that it can act as a lawyer entirely on its own and won't need (nor desire?) a human lawyer at its side.

Perhaps the only true Super Lawyer would be one that comes from the Planet Krypton (for those that don't know what that means, you need to read more comic books or watch some superhero movies).

Law As Applied To Law

Anyway, the second use case consists of the law as <u>applied to</u> AI.

Most would agree that this involves applying the law to AI in terms of overseeing or guiding or governing AI systems development, along with AI use, and encompasses the overall adoption and formulation of AI technologies.

Questions asked by those with such a focus include:

- Can or should AI systems have human rights?

- Do present laws that pertain to humans extend to whatever AI is or becomes, or do we need to enact new laws?

Those working in the realm of law as applied to AI are seeking to answer or address those kinds of problematic questions.

Conclusion

As you can see, both of the possible "AI and Law" facets are crucial, and whether you are interested in the law as <u>applied to</u> AI, or the use of AI as <u>applied to</u> law, you have your hands full with a lot of intriguing and at times gut-wrenching aspects to consider.

For this book, the focus is on AI as applied to the law.

Thus, one book, one major topic.

If you enjoy this book, please be on the look for a second book that I'm composing on the law as applied to AI.

For the moment, sit back and enjoy and be realistically informed about the herein focus of AI as applied to law.

———

Note: *For supplemental materials depicting the aspects discussed in this chapter, refer to Appendix B, which contains various augmented diagrams, charts, and additional related facets of relevance.*

See *Chapter 1 visuals on Figure 1 (page 167)*

CHAPTER 2
LEGALTECH
VERSUS LAWTECH

CHAPTER 2

LEGALTECH
VERSUS LAWTECH

Let's discuss the latest about tech as applied to the law.

There's your everyday vanilla tech, and then there's your state-of-the-art AI tech.

Best to start with the vanilla tech.

We'll do so to gradually make our way up to the vaunted topic of AI tech and the law, but first, consider the advent of everyday vanilla tech to the law.

As mentioned in the first chapter, just as MedTech refers to medical applications of technology, and FinTech involves financial applications of technology, the keywords of LegalTech and LawTech refer to the application of technology to the law.

Why does the legal or law field end-up with two monikers rather than only one?

That's a worthy question.

Be aware though that the legal or law field isn't the only one in such a predicament.

There are those that argue about MedTech versus HealthTech, and whether those are the same or differ from each other.

In some sense, the same kind of debate is occurring about the phrasing or meaning of LegalTech versus the phrasing or meaning of LawTech.

Some believe that LegalTech and LawTech are the same, and therefore you can use LegalTech or LawTech in fully interchangeable ways, as much as you like, whenever you like.

Many in fact do so.

The general popular media doesn't seem to be aware that the two monikers have any differences.

Headlines and articles about any kind of law and tech combination are likely to use either LegalTech or LawTech as labeling, interchangeably, unaware that some believe there are important differences between the two.

Experts claim they are different, which I'll explain next.

By the way, I'm not going to get bogged down herein in a debate about whether there needs to be two such names in the field of law and tech. In practical terms, there are two, and insiders cling to that belief, rather ardently.

Defining LegalTech Versus LawTech

I first will describe LegalTech and then next describe LawTech.

No order or sequence in such a discussion is intended, and they are both of equal weight and bearing.

In the minds of experts in these matters, they tend to say that LegalTech deals with tech that's for those that practice law.

Thus, any tech that supports or enables a law office or practice would be called LegalTech.

Likewise, any tech that is used by lawyers in the course of their legal pursuits would be considered LegalTech.

When the staff or legal assistants for a law firm are using tech, this would also be known as making use of LegalTech.

With that aspect hopefully made relatively clear, consider next the meaning of LawTech.

LawTech is tech that aids non-lawyers and other non-law-professionals to carry out legal or law-related tasks.

For example, some believe that any kind of self-serve legal kiosk type of system, perhaps one that allows a non-lawyer to craft a legal contract, falls into the category of LawTech.

Businesses that aren't law practices and that undertake legal or law-related tasks, not as their core competency but as something that's an aside or peripheral to the nature of their business, and done by non-lawyers, they would presumably use LawTech, assuming that they wanted to undertake law-related tasks without the use or benefit of a living breathing attorney.

In-house counsel within a business would use LegalTech, since they are in the legal profession, while if a firm allowed its HR team to perform legal-oriented tasks on their own, the HR group might be using LawTech.

So, LegalTech is for the law specialists, while LawTech is for the non-lawyer layperson.

Do you like the distinction between LegalTech and LawTech?

Some love it, while others think it is wholly unnecessary and quite confusing to try and make those distinctions.

Time will tell whether the dividing line persists or fades away.

Conclusion

How truly distinct are those two monikers of LegalTech and LawTech?

Well, it can get darned overlapping and confounding at times.

Why should a lawyer be precluded from using a system that is labeled as LawTech, and though presumably intended for laymen, yet possibly still nonetheless useful to a trained and experienced barrister?

If a lawyer does use LawTech, does it ergo need to get reclassified as being LegalTech?

Here's another twist.

Suppose a law firm purchases a LegalTech system for their practice, and it includes capabilities for their clients, allowing some clients to do a certain amount of self-serve.

In that case, is the system a LegalTech one or a LawTech one, or can it be both at the same time?

Yes, those are all valid questions.

As I say, I'm not going to engage in this rancorous debate.

It is, what it is.

For ease of reference in this book, I'm going to focus on LegalTech.

That being said, and as mentioned, there is a lot of overlap and ambiguousness between what is LegalTech and what is LawTech, thus, you can consider that some or much of what is described herein can apply to LawTech too.

Admittedly, the mainstay of the focus here is going to be about LegalTech, in its purest sense, I suppose, and so using LegalTech as the dominant keyword does make sense in this context.

Apples versus oranges, or are they roses of merely a different variety, you decide.

Note: *For supplemental materials depicting the aspects discussed in this chapter, refer to Appendix B, which contains various augmented diagrams, charts, and additional related facets of relevance.*

See Chapter 2 visuals on Figure 2 (page 169)

CHAPTER 3
DIGITAL TRANSFORMATION OF LEGAL PRACTICES

CHAPTER 3
DIGITAL TRANSFORMATION
OF LEGAL PRACTICES

If you run a legal practice or have recently set up a law office, you likely know that things are afoot due to the advent of digital technologies.

It is lore within the legal profession that law firms have often been the last to come into the digital era.

Indeed, many law firms are still using older tech that today is hard to even keep running, or for which nobody knows why or what the archaic tech does or is supposed to do.

What's even scarier, perhaps, involves law practices that cling to older tech and don't realize that some of it have been compromised in terms of well-known computer security flaws, allowing that at any moment, a curious or determined hacker could barge into the firm and see, modify, or take precious legal documents, doing so from thousands of miles away on the other side of the planet.

A hacker's paradise.

Not good.

Any head of a law practice would have to be living in a cave to not know that there is a plethora of digital capabilities now available and coming onto the market at a blazing pace.

That being said, even if they were aware of the tsunami of LegalTech, it can be quite bewildering and overwhelming.

Why pay for some darned piece of new software when, by gosh, the old-fashioned way of doing law has been sufficient for all these many years?

And, what about the cost?

Indeed, it is prudent to carefully consider what value or benefit any investment in LegalTech will derive and compare it mindfully to the costs involved to get there.

Plus, costs can be at times sneaky.

If you buy a LegalTech software package, there are all the added costs to get it up and going.

You might need added hardware, including newer servers and desktops, or perhaps newer laptops or mobile devices.

Keeping the system running is another cost.

Also, consider the learning curve aspects, such as there's the cost of your lawyers and legal teams learning to use the stuff, taking them away from otherwise billable hours.

And so on.

Cloud-based LegalTech has made the barrier to entry lower, though once again there are a slew of potential unexpected costs that will nonetheless arise even if you are using outsourced hardware.

Pushback by some law firms is rather strong to blunt or defer the allure of LegalTech.

Law partners in some firms are only going to be forced into the modern digital era by kicking and screaming, either because they do so or someone else does so to them.

Pundits say that there's a digital transformation taking place for the practice of law, and thus too for law practices, and you can't turn the clock back or somehow freeze in place while the transformation is here and gaining momentum.

Key Factors Applying Pressures

Here are some factors applying pressures:

- LegalTech emergence
- Push for data-driven legal analytics
- Enterprise apps and suites for Law Offices
- Professional Conduct adherence
- Next-Gen tech-savvy lawyers
- Need for deep legal research and reasoning
- Global work-from-anywhere (networks)
- AI proclaimed shake-up's

In a few moments, I'll dive into the LegalTech emergence.

And, then I'll dig into the AI proclaimed shake-ups.

First, though, let's consider the other pressures, giving them a little bit of attention, just to ensure that it is abundantly clear that there are many factors all converging onto the law, law practices, lawyers, and the like.

It's a grand convergence, as it were.

Can you feel the pressure?

If you are in the law field or aiming to get into it, yes, the pressure ought to be leaning on you, forcibly so, right now.

Push for Data-Driven Legal Analytics

Gone are the days of legal hunches, or so it seems.

In today's world, it's all about data.

To render a legal opinion or to run a law office, either way, you've got to have data.

Lots of data.

Data to support your contention or argument.

Data to showcase that you have your act together.

Data, data, data.

Digital tech loves data.

If you are relying on data that's amassed in loose-leaf papers and non-digital formats, you are decidedly at a disadvantage of being able to access the data, crunch the data, and analyze the data.

Once you get your data into a digital realm, the effort and cost to manage the data will radically shift, doing away with the otherwise highly laborious means, and provide new avenues to leverage and exploit the data.

As usual, there is no free lunch.

The easier it is to have data at your fingertips, the greater the chances that someone else or something else can clobber it or expose it or partake with it.

Being data-driven also carries with it the responsibility of being data-safe too.

Enterprise Apps and Suites for Law Offices

The quiet and unassuming law practice that was run by the seat-of-the-pants is falling by the wayside.

Furthermore, it used to be that to get a full suite of digital capabilities for your law office was hard to find and difficult to put into use.

Not so much, anymore.

Gradually, enterprise-oriented apps and suites for the full gamut of law office activities have emerged, and by being available in the cloud, it has reduced the arduous nature of dealing with having to set up your own internal server farm and extensive networking system.

Nonetheless, many law firms are still reluctant to let go of their own hardware and leery of breaches that can happen to publicly available cloud-based systems.

They are right in some respects and wrong in other respects.

Presumably, a proper cloud-based provider can hire and retain top computer security experts to keep the cloud offerings on a tightly woven basis and continually deal with the non-stop cat-and-mouse games of cyber hackers.

This substantive cost can be distributed across the wide swath of their cloud-using customers.

Meanwhile, most law practices would likely find it overly expensive to do the same for their own idiosyncratic setup, and as such, can be a drain too of attention toward other matters beyond those of keeping their LegalTech systems free from break-ins.

Does this make the cloud a no-brainer?

No.

Here's the rub.

Those that have gone to the cloud have at times done so without much awareness of what they are doing.

As such, there is a fine line between being in the cloud and still having to be astute enough to manage your cloud-based systems and data.

Cloud providers have often balked when a breach occurred, pointing to the cloud customer that allowed their own data to be readily accessed, failing to undertake proper precautions on their own.

The point being that just because you might switch to the cloud does not somehow make the system side of thing go away entirely or otherwise be invulnerable to neglect.

Professional Conduct Adherence

There seems to be a lot of handwringing of late about the professional conduct practices for the legal field.

New codes of professional conduct (or, more aptly stated, revisions or updates) are being considered and at times implemented.

Some fervently believe that any modern-day code of conduct ought to include a provision for being tech aware or tech-savvy as a legal professional.

The ABA some eight years ago added into the Model Rules of Professional Conduct an indication that lawyers have a duty to be competent in technology, and the latest version states this (in Rule 1.1, comment 8):

"To maintain the requisite knowledge and skill, a lawyer should keep abreast of changes in the law and its practice, including the benefits and risks associated with relevant technology, engage in continuing study and education and comply with all continuing legal education requirements to which the lawyer is subject."

Some believe that the portion of "including the benefits and risks associated with relevant technology" is helpful and well-needed.

Others say it is watered-down and insufficient.

Being aware of the benefits and risks of relevant tech is not enough, since it presumably allows being rather aloof, and some argue that lawyers should be required to go more deeply and need to know how the tech works and what it's range of capabilities consists of.

There is also angst over the wording of "relevant tech" since it is ambiguous, allowing lawyers (and, presumably, especially lawyers) to drive a Mack truck through the loophole it creates, namely, what is the scope of "relevant" and does it ergo allow lawyers that opt to flaunt the rule to say that they didn't know or don't believe that some tech X or Y was relevant to them.

Anyway, there are pressures of all kinds that are found in the ever-changing set of rules of professional conduct for the legal profession, regardless of whether they are tech-related or not.

Here's another angle.

The use of digital technology can provide a means to gauge whether professional codes of conduct are being observed by the law practice.

In addition, digital systems can advise when a potential action might be borderline or opt to go across the line.

This can be insightful for any lawyer, along with important to a law practice, for which if there is a "bad apple" in the barrel, it could taint the entire practice, thus, the sooner or more readily that a professional conduct violation is detected, the better.

Next-Gen Tech-Savvy Lawyers

Newly minted lawyers come into the marketplace and many are armed to the teeth with tech-savviness.

Not all are since some law schools are still in the dark ages, but, anyway, it's hard to undermine someone that goes to law school and already has tech in their blood, perhaps being considered even a digital native (someone that grew-up using tech).

The point is that when law firms hire newly minted lawyers, the odds are that those newbies are going to know about tech, and have an expectation of using tech.

If a law practice doesn't have modern tech, it can frustrate those tech-savvy lawyers, including that some might not join a tech-backward firm, or find themselves frustrated when being at one and ultimately be watching the clock to make the jump to another firm that has their LegalTech act together.

I'd say another worrisome aspect involves those tech-savvy lawyers that join a firm and decide to take matters into their own hands, opting to try and use tech when the firm otherwise isn't ready for it.

At first glance, you might think this is admirable and why not let the newbie adopt tech and for which the firm will presumably benefit.

Yes, and no.

The no side of things is that this effort to use tech can be done in a shadow-like way, attempting to do things underground within the law practice, or have kludge-like aspects that will ultimately come to haunt everyone involved.

What happens once that lawyer leaves the practice?

Will those remaining know what it is or how to use it?

The bottoms-up way of having tech organically grow in a firm is usually not wise, and likely to produce a mess.

In any case, there are pressures on law practices to figure out what to do about their tech-savvy lawyers.

Ironically, the usual attention goes toward those that are lacking in tech-savviness, the lawyers that are techno-illiterate, and the assumption is that tech-savvy lawyers will fend for themselves.

Whether a lawyer is on top of tech or buried beneath it, they each have their own set of requirements and needs.

Need for Deep Legal Research and Reasoning

The law keeps growing and growing.

Doing research on tough legal issues isn't quite as straightforward as it once was.

Finding a needle in a haystack is hard to do.

Furthermore, using that found needle, and combining it with other needles, and putting together a cogent legal argument, well, that's tough to do too.

As will be discussed, digital tech is aiming to help, including in some ways being able to craft legal arguments or perform legal reasoning, using AI.

Global Work-From-Anywhere (Networks)

A mon-and-pop law office today is often not on a convenient street corner where all the legal talent comes to work each morning.

We are used to the idea that large-scale law practices are spread around the globe.

Surprisingly, for some, the smallest legal practices can now be in the same boat.

No need to live and work in one specific geographical spot to come together as a legal team.

Find the best talent, and retain the best talent, regardless of where they might be.

The only reasonable way to do this involves digital tech.

If your legal team is scattered hither and yon, you've got to be using digital tech, and something robust enough to cope with the needs of a work-from-anywhere workforce of lawyers and legal assistants.

Pressures to enable this is ongoing and can be expected to rise.

LegalTech Emergence

Now that I've covered most of the other pressure factors, time to focus on the heart of this discussion, LegalTech.

LegalTech is digital technology-oriented toward and applied to law firms, lawyers, and those in legal practices, for which the tech is intended to be instrumental toward and integral to the practice of the law and the performance of legal services.

That's at least my definition, and I realize some might quibble with aspects of it.

Go with me on it, for now.

Read any of the press that covers the latest nuances of the law and the legal profession and you are going to find numerous references to some whizbang LegalTech that's taking the industry by storm.

Disruption in the legal field is being birthed each day.

The number of new apps for lawyers and law practices is doubling and tripling each year.

Yikes!

It is daunting, and not all of those apps are going to survive, yet the gist is that there is a need for new kinds of apps and LegalTech is hot and trending.

Of the trends in LegalTech, AI is certainly at the top or near to it.

AI Proclaimed Shake-ups

There is vanilla LegalTech, which can be quite exciting and offer tremendous value.

Yet, very little of it has yet been emboldened or embraced with the use of AI, which will ramp things up tremendously.

Don't misconstrue that point.

Even without AI included, LegalTech still has bona fide and crucial merit.

The icing on the cake is the AI.

That's the notion for now, though the odds are that in a few years, the AI won't be the icing anymore and will instead be either the cake itself (meaning that it is essential), or it will be cooked into the cake and icing, such that it is all part of the cake (and expected to be there).

AI is coming to legal town, slowly, gradually, and for some with great expectations, while for others with concern and consternation.

Two Camps Involved

There are two camps about the advent of AI in the legal profession.

One camp believes that it is about time and that AI will augment lawyers, adding to the arsenal of legal tools at their disposal.

A newbie lawyer will essentially have a fellow seasoned "machine" lawyer at their beck and call, allowing them to use the AI as though a human lawyer could be their own special mentor or guide.

Imagine that!

A 24x7 seasoned lawyer that sits awaiting use, whenever, wherever, and however needed.

Cool.

Human lawyers could presumably do more than they otherwise could do without having at their fingertips this AI lawyer augmentation.

It would potentially make lawyers more efficient and effective, no matter whether the human lawyer using the AI was new or one that has been practicing law for decades.

This shouldn't scare lawyers; it should enthrall them, many argue.

The same can be said for law offices, aiming to embrace rather than reject AI.

Okay, that's the viewpoint about augmenting lawyers with AI.

Next, consider he perspective that AI will actually replace lawyers.

In theory, if AI is going to work the way in which it is being depicted (able to give unabashed legal advice), you could do more law work with fewer lawyers, thus, no matter how you spin things, it means fewer lawyers.

The point here is that even if AI is only an augmentation to human lawyers, you are likely to need fewer human lawyers to do a given amount of legal work, and it then cuts down on the number of lawyers needed.

The counterargument is that each lawyer can do more work, and as long as you increase the volume of work, you are still keeping whole the need for lawyers.

But is there some finite amount of work and so this kind of leaping forward game isn't especially practical?

In any case, set aside that aspect and shift toward the notion that an AI system could do everything a human lawyer could do (it's an idea, not a practicality today).

By the way, when referring to doing everything a human lawyer could do, some balk and point out that besides knowing the law, a human lawyer can provide a shoulder to cry on, and provide other *humanly* oriented aspects that an AI system is presumably not going to provide.

I don't want to go down that rabbit hole, which just to let you know, takes us to the topic of robots that can provide a shoulder to cry on, or that AI systems might be programmed to be more personable and caring than those lawyers that are tone-deaf toward empathy, etc.

Stick with the concept that an AI system could entirely replace a lawyer.

Not so good if you are a lawyer or planning on becoming one.

Should the legal profession be fighting against the advent of AI as applied to the law?

Some say yes.

Others have a different reason to fight it.

Unless the AI is so good that it can truly replace a lawyer, which seems doubtful for certainly the near-term in terms of what AI can do today (more on this later on in the book), the chances are that any AI system of a standalone nature is going to give problematic legal advice.

Allow me a moment to explain.

If an AI system cannot be fully competent for providing legal advice, it would seem best to ensure that it isn't in a posture or circumstance where it can seemingly provide legal advice on a standalone basis (meaning, without being augmented by a human lawyer).

Consider the ABA rule 1.1:

"A lawyer shall provide competent representation to a client. Competent representation requires the legal knowledge, skill, thoroughness, and preparation reasonably necessary for the representation."

Until or if AI can achieve that rule of competence, it ought not to be providing legal advice, at least on the basis of doing so without a human lawyer in the mix.

That being said, there is certainly reasonable concern that any AI that appears to be able to provide legal advice, even if emblazoned as not ready for competency, will nonetheless be used as though it is legally competent.

Thus, two formidable concerns:

1) AI that is touted as being able to replace human lawyers in their entirety will not be provable as being able to do so, raising the specter that the legal advice so given by the AI system is potentially fishy, brittle, or otherwise weaker than a human lawyer

2) AI that is touted as being able to replace human lawyers could be a boastful claim or ill-kept promise that misleads the public into a false willingness to use such AI systems, not realizing the peril it entails them (i.e., under the assumption that the AI is not able to properly and appropriately do so).

For a useful thought exercise on this topic, you might ponder the aspect of how one could "prove" that an AI system is comparable to a human lawyer in terms of being able to render legal advice.

In the AI field, there is a well-known generic method that is referred to as the Turing Test, which is used to figure out whether an AI system is able to presumably exhibit human intelligence.

In brief, the Turing Test involves setting up a situation whereby you have a human and an AI system, each separately hiding behind say a screen or a partition, and you ask questions of the two, out of which if you cannot discern which is which, the AI is then deemed as having passed the Turing Test (presumably, being undistinguishable of human intelligence as exhibited by the human).

It's a handy way to consider the matter.

There are a lot of complications and limitations though.

For example, if the person that asks the questions doesn't ask telltale questions, the aspect of being able to claim that human intelligence is exhibited by the AI is rather doubtful.

Pretend that you ask the AI and the human to tell you what two plus two is equal to.

They both say the answer is four.

You stop the test.

Has this "proven" sufficiently that the AI is exhibiting the equivalent of human intelligence?

You'd be hard-pressed to say it "proves" that the AI is the equivalent of human intelligence, since insufficient testing was undertaken to make such a brash claim.

Conclusion

There are lots of pressures facing lawyers and law offices.

Among those pressures is the advent of LegalTech.

On top of that ongoing pressure of LegalTech, we can pile on the advent of AI.

Good or bad, the use of LegalTech and the use of AI as its brethren is coming, so best to be prepared.

In short, it could be that:

1. **Augment.** Lawyers will be augmented by AI, which is useful for lawyers, yet it could also mean that in the aggregate not as many lawyers are needed since a lawyer with an AI tool could potentially do the work of those other lawyers that might otherwise have been needed to meet workload demands.

2. **Replace.** Lawyers might be replaced by AI, doing so in specific and narrow areas, thus, reducing the volume of need for human lawyers (and though some speculate about the robo-lawyer replacing human lawyers altogether, that's not in the cards for a long time to come).

If you are a lawyer and abiding by the ABA, presumably you should be keeping up on LegalTech and AI, assuring that you comply with Rule 1.1 Comment 8.

Come to think of it, I suppose that if you are reading this book, you are doing your professional duty and thus keeping your eyes wide open about what's coming down the pike in tech (good for you!).

———

Note: *For supplemental materials depicting the aspects discussed in this chapter, refer to Appendix B, which contains various augmented diagrams, charts, and additional related facets of relevance.*

See Chapter 3 visuals on Figures 3-5 (pp. 171-175)

CHAPTER 4

LEGAL ACTIVITIES FRAMEWORK

CHAPTER 4

LEGAL ACTIVITIES FRAMEWORK

As stated, LegalTech is tech that's applied to law offices, lawyers, and the like, aiding in the carrying out of legal work.

What kind of legal work or legal-related tasks do law offices, lawyers, and related staff do?

In other words, we need to put some specifics around the notion of what LegalTech is aiming to accomplish, and it is hopefully self-evident in this context that it is important to understand the range of tasks performed by those undertaking legal oriented tasks.

Consider an example of one rather everyday task, the creation of a legal contract.

A lawyer that's tasked with preparing a legal contract will likely undergo a series of steps in doing so.

First, the lawyer needs to ascertain what the basis for the contract will be, including why such a contract is needed, and to what use it is intended to be put.

Without first identifying the overall purpose, it makes little sense to just jump into crafting a contract.

The contract will need to meet various requirements, and those requirements need to be surfaced to then provide guidance toward crafting the contract.

In terms of crafting the contract, it is likely that the lawyer would take a look at other contracts that might be similar or otherwise provide narrative and content that can be reused.

No sense in starting from scratch, unless somehow the requirements are so unique that no other contract can offer any insights or reuse.

While crafting the language of the contract, the lawyer needs to self-check what they've written.

Is the language appropriate and sufficient?

Are there potential misinterpretations or guffaws that need to be dealt with before the contract is considered fully drafted?

And so on.

Let's consider a scenario where none of this contract work is being done in a digital manner.

You would need to handwrite the contract.

You'd have lots of markups and annotations for corrections and fixes.

It would be difficult to share the draft with others.

It would be arduous to get reviews from those reviewers.

You might lose touch with what the status of the draft has become.

There would not be an easy way to know what changes were made when they were made, and who made the changes.

Fortunately, I think we all accept that drafting a contract without any digital tools is fraught with all sorts of disadvantages (some of you might remember the days of typewriters, prior to the advent of readily available computers, in which case, the aforementioned scenario might bring back tears of joy or tears of despair).

With modern-day word processing and editing, nearly all of those facets of drafting a legal contract become much easier and straightforward.

That being the case, there is a difference between simpleton tech for contracts and more advanced tech for contracts.

In the next scenario, imagine tech that's specially built for contracts.

When trying to figure out if a prior contract might exist that would be pertinent to drafting this new contract, you can use an online query tool to find prior contracts.

And, not just any contract, but one that matches well to this latest matter, thus, it isn't the typical "dumb" search that just brings back anything, but could be "smart" in that it tries to find contracts related to the requirements of this new contract.

The contract drafting tech might also offer substitutions of text based on the requirements, placing those substitutions into the prior found pertinent contract that's going to be reused.

Essentially, up to the point of having to put your noggin into thinking about the meaning of the contract, the textual and narrative aspects can be handily aided via advanced tech.

There are many LegalTech apps now that will help with drafting and preparing legal contracts.

They continue to advance, making life easier and easier for the lawyer performing the contract preparation task.

That's great!

We'll revisit this example about drafting a contract when we later get to the topic of AI and LegalTech and see how AI can punch this up more so.

Okay, so there are tasks that lawyers and law offices perform, and LegalTech can help, as illuminated via the example of drafting a contract.

What else?

What other tasks are performed?

Here are the typical legal activities that are performed by lawyers and law offices:

- Case Management
- Contracts
- Courts/Trials
- Discovery
- Documents/Records
- IP
- Law Office/Practice
- Lawyer & Client Interaction
- Legal Assistants
- Legal Collaboration
- Legal Research
- Legal Workflow
- Legal Writing
- Professional Conduct
- Other

I've listed the tasks in alphabetical sequence. Doing so makes the list easier to read, plus it avoids denoting any priority of the sequence or order.

Those with a keen eye will notice that the word "Other" is shown at the end of the list, yet if the list is in alphabetical sequence, it ought to be further up.

This was done to highlight that the list itself is not considered an exhaustive list and merely a typical and semi-complete list.

There are other tasks that could be added to the list, and you are encouraged to do so.

By-and-large, the list captures many of the essential or core tasks that lawyers and law offices undertake.

Some of those tasks are relatively small-scale and can be done readily, while others are large-scale and quite complex.

What's happening within LegalTech is that inch-by-inch there is new tech being formulated and provided to the marketplace that covers this full-range of legal oriented tasks.

In some cases, the LegalTech is singular in focus and covers perhaps just one of the tasks, or maybe only part of one of the tasks.

In other cases, there is LegalTech provided in suites, consisting of a multitude of interrelated apps that cover multiple tasks.

Some suites are well-coordinated together, while others are a slam together of separate apps that aren't particularly integrated.

Though some vendors might claim they have a suite that covers everything A-to-Z, this is a doubtful claim, and furthermore, oftentimes a suite might not have the best-in-class as a tech for each and every task.

Don't misread that point.

There can be best-in-class tech for tasks within a suite.

There can though be less than best-in-class too in a suite.

There can also be best-in-class that's standalone.

This does not though mean that best-in-class tech is always found exclusively in standalone apps.

I hope that clarifies (a bit digressive, but worthwhile points).

The Rub Of Tech Versus Manual

Consider the full range of various tasks that have been listed as typical legal activities.

The odds are that any given law practice will have some mix of tech for undertaking those tasks and some amount of manual or non-automated effort used to perform those tasks.

It could be that the mix of automation and no automation are found within the performance of a particular task (intra-task).

In addition, it could be that one task has tech available, but when trying to shift the result or product from that task to another task on the list, things breakdown and you need to go the manual route rather than using tech (this deals with inter-task aspects).

Realize that this will vary depending upon any specific law office and how it has setup its tech.

In other words, law office A might be well-automated and have a slew of these tasks aided by tech, and only a few aren't aided by tech, while law office B might have very few of these tasks aided by tech.

It all depends on what approach the law firm has taken to put in place its tech.

There is nothing inherent or innate in these tasks that they could not all be aided by tech, and furthermore that the tech could not somehow integrate with all the other tech involved in performing these tasks.

Few law practices though are that tech-enabled.

It's a lot harder to achieve than it might seem on paper.

Anyway, the gist here is that there's bound to be some mix of tech and manual efforts required in nearly all law efforts and this is going to be important to keep in mind when considering how AI is going to come to the table.

Across The Hierarchy

Another way to look at the list of legal activities involves considering their use across a hierarchy of a law firm or law office.

Using a typical pyramid shape for a hierarchy, at the top is the overarching law firm or law office.

This top-level typically includes the corporate officers, executives, and leading partners of the organization.

There are the lawyers that undertake the provisioning of legal services, along with the use of legal assistants, and various staff.

And, of course, the clients for which the legal service is being undertaken.

This pyramid perspective is useful as a means to realize that legal activities have a multitude of touchpoints, ranging up and down and throughout the hierarchy.

Likewise, any LegalTech that supports or enables the legal activities is going to have those same kinds of touchpoints, and should be built to do so.

That being said, not all LegalTech is adept at being useable across and throughout all such layers of a hierarchy.

You might have a contracts app that is suitable for lawyers, but maybe not readily usable by legal assistants or staff.

You might have a case management system that is used by those within the firm, but has no access provided for clients.

And so on.

These characteristics are not necessarily based on what's needed and instead are often based on simply whatever was devised when the tech was created. Many of the existing LegalTech offerings were not devised with a big picture in mind of holistically covering all types of users in all types of uses.

Instead, most of the prevailing tech was crafted in a narrower way, and at times extended to try and go further toward meeting all user's needs.

In fact, some of the leading latest LegalTech being formulated by startups are overcoming prior constraints and touting that they provide uses for a wider variety of users.

Meanwhile, sometimes, legacy LegalTech has a harder time making changes to accommodate such needs.

Conclusion

Of course, it is not the case that all legacy LegalTech is somehow less capable than the newer LegalTech.

I'm just saying that for some of the emerging LegalTech, they were able to start with a blank slate, and considered too the drawbacks or qualms surfaced about legacy LegalTech, and thus they then were able to proceed toward crafting something newer and better that would avoid those prior pitfalls.

Note: *For supplemental materials depicting the aspects discussed in this chapter, refer to Appendix B, which contains various augmented diagrams, charts, and additional related facets of relevance.*

See Chapter 4 visuals on Figures 6-8 (pp. 177-181)

CHAPTER 5
AI AND LEGALTECH BUILDING BLOCKS

CHAPTER 5

AI AND LEGALTECH
BUILDING BLOCKS

It's time to start getting AI into this equation.

So far, we've covered that there are various legal activities that are performed by a law office or law practice, and those legal activities can be supported or enabled via LegalTech, though there are lots of potential gaps in the tech coverage, meaning that manual or non-automated efforts come to play too.

The LegalTech can be amplified or stepped-up by adding AI capabilities.

That's exciting and heartwarming.

Though, as you might recall, we've discussed the dilemma of whether AI is going to be augmenting human lawyers or potentially replacing human lawyers.

Oops, didn't mean to get things riled up again.

Let's get back to the matter at hand.

Suppose we do want to add AI to the performance of the various legal activities.

Take that as a given.

Here's the deal.

If a legal activity is being accomplished in a digital manner, via the use of some kind of LegalTech, it's going to make adding AI a lot easier than if the task is being done on a manual basis.

Generally, an AI system is going to need the underlying task to be supported by a digital foundation.

It's a leg-up.

This does not mean that you couldn't add AI to a completely to-date manual task.

The odds are though that it's going to be more arduous, likely more costly, and potentially less viable, without first getting things into a digital format.

Where there is a will, there is a way, and so not yet having automation for a task does not preclude it from being amenable to AI.

Indeed, there are potentially some tasks that might require a re-look at how they were put into a digital form, in order to then layer onto the task, the use of AI.

Having LegalTech supporting a legal activity does not imply that adding AI is a slam dunk.

The usual sequence involves getting legal activities from the manual mode into a digital LegalTech supported mode.

Then, you can build AI on top of that.

If there isn't that digital LegalTech intermediary layer, the AI needs to be leaped across the gap or divide.

This often means having to spend time and effort getting things into a digital mode.

And, this could also end-up becoming an undesirable one-off, namely that at some later point you might want to put a more robust LegalTech solution into place, and then you'll need to deal with some bridge solution that was put in place to get to the AI side.

I'm not saying don't do it.

Just emphasizing that if you are desirous of adding AI to some particular task of the legal activities, and if you don't have a LegalTech solution already in place, it might make sense to do that first.

That being said, there might be some urgency that doesn't allow you to do the LegalTech first, in which case, fine, just keep your eyes open as you proceed down the AI path.

Conclusion

Right now, it's kind of a wild west as to what's happening with the AI add-ons for legal activities.

For example, the LegalTech solution that you are using for task Q, might not be readily able to add an AI element.

Meanwhile, assume for sake of argument that some other LegalTech app does.

Do you switch from the LegalTech app that doesn't support the AI to one that does?

It's hard to say in the abstract.

It might be better to find out whether the AI is going to be added to the LegalTech solution, and if so, when and how.

Also, how crucial is that AI add-on to your use?

Until we reach a tipping point of AI for LegalTech, it's all a hit-or-miss proposition.

Let's proceed further into what AI consists of, allowing us to consider what value or benefit might be derived by the addition of AI into LegalTech and/or the performance of legal activities.

Note: *For supplemental materials depicting the aspects discussed in this chapter, refer to Appendix B, which contains various augmented diagrams, charts, and additional related facets of relevance.*

See Chapter 5 visuals on Figures 9-10 (pp. 183-185)

CHAPTER 6
AI FUNDAMENTALS

CHAPTER 6

AI FUNDAMENTALS

AI is coming, AI is coming.

But what is it?

Let's answer that question in this chapter.

AI is really two aspects at once:

1. **Seek to have machines artificially achieve human intelligence**

2. **Do #1 via the use of various technologies (an umbrella of tech to achieve AI aspirations or goals)**

You have to be willing to put your mind toward the notion that AI is simultaneously a goal or aspiration, along with thinking of it as some kind of technology that is trying to achieve that goal or aspiration.

This is a <u>crucial</u> duality to keep in mind, at all times.

I say this because there is a great deal of confusion about AI, especially as depicted in mass media.

The overarching goal or aspiration for those in AI is to devise a machine or machines that artificially achieve human intelligence.

When I refer to a machine, consider that to be a computer, since computers are the most likely candidate for getting us to the artificially developed human-like intelligence.

We might someday develop something other than a computer, which I'll call an other-thing, and maybe that's the "machine" that gets us to the vaunted goal of AI, but for now, we'll assume that the cornerstone is a computer of one type or another.

Arriving at AI that is akin to human intelligence is a tall order.

A really tall order.

Mega-tall.

We aren't there yet.

This is where the duality that I've asked you to keep in your mind will now come to play.

There is a Darwinian race right now of trying to forge technologies that will achieve AI.

Some of the tech will maybe get us there, some maybe not.

Nobody yet knows.

I'll refer to that set of technologies as an umbrella of such technologies.

Many elements within the umbrella are known by the aspects that they each contribute toward achieving AI, while some of them aren't necessarily considered on the path to AI per se and have their own path.

Some experts on AI fervently believe in allowing anything and everything, inclusive of the kitchen sink, as being a proper member to be tossed into or under the umbrella, if it will somehow get us a step closer to reaching true AI.

As such, I suppose you could list not only topics traditionally found in computer science, but you can add all other sciences, such as physics, biology, chemistry, and you could include other seemingly disparate subjects, including anthropology, psychology, and so on, any of which might provide the last straw to finally help break the camel's back of achieving true AI.

Traditionally, here's the core technologies and subfields of study that seem to belong in AI-proper (meaning, the aspects most people think of as AI relevant):

- Machine Learning (ML)

- Knowledge-Based Systems (KBS)

- Natural Language Processing (NLP)

- Computer Vision (CV)

- Robotics / Autonomy

- Common-Sense Reasoning

- Other Technologies

The ubiquitous "Other Technologies" allow this list to exist without excessive criticism that something vital is being left off the list.

We'll be taking a deeper look at these AI technologies in the next chapter.

Is It The Real McCoy Or Something Else

We know that the goal of AI is to achieve a machine that artificially exhibits human intelligence, and for which we are going to keep as a high bar that the artificially instantiated intelligence is akin to the highest levels that we hold human intelligence to.

Thus, if you made a machine that was as intelligent as a rat, yes, that would nifty, but it isn't the goal that we are aiming at for AI overall.

You'd have fallen short, though maybe provided a steppingstone for the next level or levels of AI attainment.

Let's divide the approach to achieving true AI into two camps (a favorite way to carve up things).

The goal of AI can be achieved by either of:

1. **Replicate:** Try to replicate how the human brain works, and therefore presumably arrive at the equivalent of human intelligence, or

2. **Alternative:** Devise some other means altogether to showcase human intelligence

In the replicate approach, you aim to build a replica of the human brain, using computers to do so, and voila, hopefully, it will produce human intelligence, and presumably human intelligence that is akin to the levels of human intelligence in everyday humans.

If you did the replicate approach and ended up with the same intelligence as a rat or a rabbit, something must have gotten cross-wired since the result should have been human intelligence.

Notice that we're not saying that the machine is a human at that point, it is only exhibiting the same as human intelligence

Some believe that if we did achieve human intelligence in a box, maybe that thing or him or her ought to then get human rights.

That's a fight for another day and would take us over into the other side of the AI-and-Law coin, namely the topic of the law applied to AI (recall, this was briefly discussed in the opening chapter).

The replicate approach seems to be somewhat promising due to the advent of Machine Learning (ML), a method of mimicking some aspects of the brain, though as we'll cover in the next chapter, we are still zillions of miles away from achieving true human intelligence using the ML method.

One aspect to clarify here is that if the AI was indeed achieved in some machine, via the replicate approach, there would be an essential requirement that the machine is pretty much the same as the properties of the human brain, minus necessarily being biological in the same manner as the human brain.

Some would assert that you would be simulating the brain, doing so in a likewise manner of the brain, and therefore the thing or the "it" is not an actual brain, though perhaps an impressive mimicry of it.

That sounds like an insult or a complaint, but pretty much anyone that could arrive at human intelligence via a machine that happens to replicate the human brain, well, I dare say they aren't going to care much about whether you are willing to call their creation a brain or not.

We'd all be too busy giving them a Nobel Prize.

Here's another way to consider the matter.

I get all the Lego pieces that I can find (yes, I'm referring to the toy puzzle pieces), and I miraculously assemble them into being a machine that exhibits the same level of intelligence as humans.

If I assembled them in such a way that it was based on how the human brain seems to work, including that the pieces were formed into neuron-like elements, and so on, it would be considered as based on the replicate approach.

There is an alternative way to do things.

If I assemble the pieces in some other manner, which I'm not going to tell you how, since you would run out and make one and I'd not get the Noble Prize while you would, and the assembled thing was able to exhibit human intelligence, it would be considered in the alternative approach bracket.

Now that you know of these two approaches, ask yourself, which one will win the race to AI.

Are you better off by trying to figure out how the brain works and replicate it into a machine?

That seems sensible and prudent.

You know that a brain is able to achieve human intelligence, therefore, you must be on the right path if you are taking the replicate approach.

Seems obvious.

Of course, suppose there are some tricks to the human brain that we won't be able to crack for a thousand years, in which case, your machine is going to not arise until after that thousand years mark.

Or, suppose we never crack the code of the human brain.

Your AI goal won't ever be achieved, at least on the basis of the purist version of the replicate approach.

You presumably are dependent upon first figuring out the human brain.

Brains are rather inscrutable.

You've set yourself a hurdle that might not be hurdled.

The alternative camp says that maybe we don't need to know how the brain works, or maybe we might know just enough that it helps us part of the way to achieving human intelligence, and yet we come up with some other solution that drives us home the rest of the way.

This sounds convincing.

Unfortunately, suppose that the alternative approach is going in the wrong direction, and yet you might not know that it is.

You have no apriori means to ascertain for sure that the alternative approach is going to arrive at human intelligence, which, by the very nature of the approach, comes with the approach.

In short, you would be trying to discover how to give rise to human intelligence via means and methods that you likely have no idea will really produce that result.

Some would call this a shot-in-the-dark Hail Mary.

On the other hand, if the replicate is going to get jammed-up by not figuring out the human brain, maybe the alternative approach has the upper hand, as it were, and might leap past those that are stuck on looking at one brain after another.

I hope you found this discussion interesting.

If you were to now ask me which approach is the "right one," I'm afraid I'd have to ask you to go and sit in the back of the class and think carefully about what you've just said, and perhaps read this chapter again.

Nobody knows.

From the perspective of AI as applied to the law, admittedly this debate over the replicate versus the alternative is somewhat abstract and not something that will make the difference about applying AI to LegalTech and legal activities, certainly not in the near-term.

Nonetheless, it's useful for you to know, and thus be on your toes when someone makes a bold claim that they've found or landed on true AI.

Be skeptical and start asking probing questions.

More Than Human Intelligence

Do you think that humanity will be satisfied if it is possible to arrive at AI?

If a machine could exhibit human intelligence, would we become quite pleased with ourselves and relish such an amazing accomplishment?

Probably not.

Some believe that we'd want to go further, going beyond the mere achieving of human intelligence.

We might aim to achieve Super-Intelligence.

Indeed, we might craft **Artificial Super-Intelligence (ASI)**, which seems notable and a job well done.

Exceeded expectations.

What would ASI do?

Nobody can say.

Perhaps because we are limited to our human intelligence and cannot see beyond human intelligence to anticipate what a greater intelligence would consist of.

That being said, there are lots of science fiction writers that have tried to predict what Super-Intelligence might be. Sometimes those depictions are about alien beings that come to earth or that we meet in space, while other times the depictions are of artificial versions.

Anyway, most people in AI agree that the time at which we might somehow achieve conventional true AI, the kind that accomplishes (mere) human intelligence, including being sentient (ill-defined!), has a name to it, specifically, it is referred to as the point of **singularity**.

Are you afraid of singularity?

Sure, I am, since we don't know what this AI thing might do.

Are you eager for singularity?

Sure, I am, since we might find ourselves with a new buddy.

For the moment, aiming at human intelligence is pretty good and we don't need to have a stretch goal in mind.

But it could be that we overshoot and arrive at ASI, inadvertently, accidentally.

Once again, we don't know if that's a good thing or a bad thing since the ASI might decide to essentially squish us like a bug, believing that we are no better than ants.

Alternatively, the ASI might be grateful for being created by us and opt to use all its intellectual powers for the betterment of mankind

The thing is, suppose that we didn't intend to arrive at ASI.

Some are worried that our efforts to achieve AI, the conventional AI, the singularity, might go awry and catapult into ASI.

Would ASI be grateful when we hadn't planned for the ASI ascension?

Here's a twist upon the twist.

Imagine if there's something beyond ASI, embodying super-duper Super-Intelligence.

Might we end-up there?

Well, since there's no clear demarcation of the endpoint of ASI, it's hard to say that there's anything beyond it since the beyond part might be considered part-and-parcel of ASI to begin with.

Some More AI Vocab

While we are on the topic of AI and the singularity, along with ASI (be forewarned that "ASI" is a rarely used abbreviation, and most just say "super-intelligence" rather than referring to the abbreviated version), it is handy to introduce some additional helpful AI vocabulary.

I've tried to emphasize that we are not anywhere close to achieving true AI, which, as a reminder, consists of the goal of arriving at artificial human intelligence in all its respects.

Meanwhile, in specific domains, there are some interesting AI applications that do well at seemingly exhibiting very narrow human-like intelligence, though please think of the word narrow as being in all caps and bolded, like this **NARROW**.

I say that because people keep referring to these small-scale variants of AI as "narrow AI" and yet this is taking liberty with the true AI aspirations.

You might think that the word "narrow" simply means that the AI application is say an AI system that can do what a medical doctor can do though in a narrow field such as diagnosing diseases based on looking at MRI's.

Thus, it purports or implies that it is AI narrowed to a particular domain or subdomain.

That's not the truth about the word "narrow" as used in this context.

Narrow means a lot more of narrowness, a heaping of narrowness.

The narrow AI applications aren't at all like human intelligence and are completely lacking for example in any semblance of common-sense reasoning.

No matter what you might say about medical doctors, you'd have to admit they have common-sense reasoning, even if it's a different sense of common-sense from your own, you'd still agree they have it, yet these narrow AI applications in the medical domain don't have common-sense reasoning.

Do I want a narrow AI to help my medical doctor to figure out if my MRI is presenting something untoward?

Sure, of course.

There's no doubt that in some instances the AI is going to be more methodical, more detailed, less prone to getting tired or making mistakes.

Those narrow AI applications though don't have and aren't exhibiting human intelligence in the aspirational way of true AI.

Not yet.

The use of the AI moniker has gotten quite out-of-hand and it seems that everyone loves to claim they have "AI" regardless of what their system does or cannot do.

This has made it harder for people within AI to speak of the true AI, and thus, there's another handy acronym that some like to use, namely **Artificial General Intelligence (AGI).**

The heathens can use the "AI" moniker for whatever they wish, and misuse it, but those on the inside know that when those barbarians refer to AI, it might be the true AI aspirational goal or it might be something lesser so.

With the use of AGI, you are able to immediately indicate that you are referring to the true AI.

AGI would include common-sense reasoning, along with whatever else is going to be needed to arrive at true AI.

There is something else that also sometimes comes up in the halls of AI. Some like to contemplate and discuss the potential for an **intelligence explosion.**

Here's what that signifies.

Some assert that intelligence begets intelligence.

The more you have, the more it can spark additional intelligence.

If that's the case, perhaps when crafting AI, we might not need to fully do all the work ourselves, and it could be that with the right minimal amount of AI, the rest of the artificial intelligence will produce itself, doing so in a chain reaction manner.

The intelligence chain reaction is usually called the intelligence explosion.

It sure would be nice if we only had to do one-half the job and the rest of the intelligence would fill itself in. Or, maybe we only need to do one-tenth of the job. Perhaps only one-millionth of the job.

Nobody knows.

There is a rub.

If the intelligence explosion gets underway, and we don't know how to control it, might this be the means by which we arrive at ASI or whatever comes after ASI?

Conclusion

Those of you that are history buffs might know that during the making of the atomic bomb, there was concern among some of the scientists that it might start a chain reaction that would be unstoppable by human means.

One theory was that the air would ignite, and this would happen rapidly, spreading around the entire globe, causing a conflagration that would wipe-out anything living on earth.

Might an artificial intelligence explosion provide an intelligence that could then wipe-out anything living on earth?

Maybe.

I'll go with the glass is half-full and suggest that it would provide intelligence allowing us to solve all of humanity's most pressing problems.

Hope that helps you sleep at night.

Note: *For supplemental materials depicting the aspects discussed in this chapter, refer to Appendix B, which contains various augmented diagrams, charts, and additional related facets of relevance.*

See Chapter 6 visuals on Figures 11-14 (pp. 187-193)

CHAPTER 7

TAXONOMY OF
AI TECHNOLOGIES

CHAPTER 7

TAXONOMY OF AI TECHNOLOGIES

Here again are the core technologies and subfields of study that seem to belong in AI-proper (meaning the aspects most people think of as AI relevant):

- Machine Learning (ML)

- Knowledge-Based Systems (KBS)

- Natural Language Processing (NLP)

- Computer Vision (CV)

- Robotics / Autonomy

- Common-Sense Reasoning

- Other Technologies

And, as a convenient reminder, the ubiquitous "Other Technologies" allows this list to exist without excessive criticism that something vital is being left off the list.

I'm going to use this list of core technologies and subfields as a taxonomy for AI.

To be clear, there are lots of ways to categorize and provide a taxonomy of AI.

Furthermore, they all tend to vary since it isn't like a taxonomy of animals or something that is pretty much well-specified and bounded.

You'll need to go with the flow on this, and so let's move on.

There are specialists in each of these subdomains of AI.

If you were going to hire an AI developer, you'd want to find out what specialty they are versed in.

Don't assume that all AI developers are versed in all aspects of AI.

Not likely.

If this seems odd to you, pretend that you were going to hire a plumber.

Would you expect the plumber to also be an electrician?

I don't think so.

You might get a general contractor that knows something about plumbing, electrical wiring, and so on, and in that same way of thinking, if you seek to get an AI person, there are some that are akin to a general contractor.

The odds are that the general contractor is not your best choice for doing the plumbing, and so you'd still undoubtedly want to find a plumber, and fortunately, the general contractor would likely know what a plumber does and how to pick one and how to make sure the plumber is doing a good job.

The same is the case for AI.

There are AI specialists in Machine Learning.

There are AI specialists in Natural Language Processing.

There are AI specialists in Robotics.

And so on.

Few would be considered a specialist or expert in all areas of AI.

In today's application of AI, you'll find that most AI applications tend to use one of the subdomains and not much of the other subdomains.

For example, a contract analysis app that uses AI is probably using aspects of Natural Language Processing, and maybe not any of the other AI subdomains.

It's hard to know until you ask someone what their AI consists of.

Plus, you'd want to get under-the-hood or do something to try and verify what they claim.

A more robust use of AI would be to combine together several of the AI subdomain's capabilities.

This is often referred to as an **ensemble** version of AI.

Part of the reason that you don't see that much of ensemble AI is due to my point about the fact that many in AI tend to gravitate toward a particular subdomain.

As such, someone that knows how to use a hammer uses it for whatever problem arises, even if it involves not hammering nails but instead trying to put in screws.

Gradually, we'll see more and more AI applications that go beyond the hammer perspective and embrace a multitude of AI subdomains.

You might be wondering what kinds of stuff goes into the Other Technologies category?

I'd put a hodgepodge of things in there.

One aspect would be **Distributed AI (DAI),** which is a subdomain involving trying to distribute AI capabilities and yet have them work together in a coordinated fashion.

This is used in swarms.

For example, you might have drones that are each using some form of AI on-board the computer that's running the flying drone.

In addition, the drones might work together in a coordinated fashion, using DAI to guide their collective or swarm-like movements.

Not yet something especially relevant to AI as applied to the law, but perhaps one day in the future.

Anyway, the point being that the core technologies that I've listed are the primary ones that you hear about or that are used in "every day" AI applications, meanwhile there's a slew of other stuff that's being cooked-up in AI research labs.

Machine Learning (ML)

There's no doubt that Machine Learning is the 300-pound gorilla of AI technologies today.

Everyone is agog over Machine Learning.

Unfortunately, as yet another indication of the naming of things, the wording of "machine" and "learning" suggests greater powers and capabilities than is currently the case.

Essentially, today's ML is computational pattern matching.

For those of you that have familiarity with statistics, you can think of ML as part of the overall statistical algorithm's family.

Indeed, most would include the statistical technique of regression as a member of the ML realm.

Though there are various conventional statistical techniques in ML, the greatest acclaim and attention would seem to go toward the use of Artificial Neural Networks (ANNs), something that you would likely not know or realize is yet another kind of statistical approach, albeit different than conventional methods.

ANNs are a simulation of sorts, attempting to borrow the notion of neurons, and by using those simulated "neurons" in a collective way, thus formed into a network or collective of them, you can do some interesting pattern detection.

Not everyone refers to the use of these computationally calculated "neurons" as Artificial Neural Networks (I do), and instead use the easier "Neural Networks" to refer to such computer-based systems, but I like using the word "artificial" to help distinguish that these are not the biological versions of neurons and neural networks.

Importantly, these simulated NN's (ANN's, more properly) aren't yet anything close to what real neurons and real NN's are.

Some hope that perhaps ultimately we'll be able to create extremely large-scale ANNs and make them more akin to the biological version in our heads, which might get us closer to achieving true AI (via the replicate notion that has been covered in the prior chapter).

When using an ANN that is somewhat smaller, you can't get as much out of it in terms of the pattern matching robustness, so the notion is to increase the number of neurons (artificial) and the size and potentially shape of the network (the artificial neural network), including how the neurons are interconnected, aiming to make the whole thing larger and larger enough for improved capabilities.

To distinguish shallow or smaller ANNs from larger ANNs, most refer to the larger ones as showcasing **Deep Learning**.

There isn't a magic number that everyone agrees is the demarcation between being Deep Learning versus something less so (nobody wants to own up to having Shallow Learning or Scant Learning, but that can be the case), and instead, it's one of those beauty is in the eye-of-the-beholder aspects.

There are a variety of elements and aspects of Machine Learning that are useful to be aware of.

These are some of the more popular and significant aspects of Machine Learning:
- ML Frameworks Used
- Deep Learning (DL)
- Artificial Neural Networks (ANN)
- Supervised Models
- Unsupervised Models
- Reinforcement Models
- Explainability (XAI)
- Data Requirements
- Training Requirements
- Prediction Capabilities
- Base Algorithms
- Clustering
- Regression
- Analytics
- Real-Time
- Scalability
- Etc.

During the earlier days of ML, much of the building of an ML involved doing computer programming and was somewhat arcane to accomplish.

Nowadays, there many software packages that have the ML modeling capabilities available.

Besides specialized ML software packages, most of the major statistics packages that you might already know have added many of the ML modeling constructs.

When you think about statistical packages, you usually right away also realize that you need to have data to be able to adequately use a statistical routine.

Any statistics class emphasizes that you need to have sufficient and proper data to calculate stats, and also need to think carefully about the nature of the data, including whether it contains inherent biases, how the data was collected, the accuracy of the data values, and so on.

All of that is the same for ML.

Unfortunately, partially since ML modeling has become so easy due to the availability of ML modeling packages, there are many that are crafting ML models that aren't particularly sound and have forgotten or neglected the basic principles espoused when determining statistics.

Anyway, in the case of using ML for legal activities, keep in mind that it is easier to do than might otherwise seem, but doing it properly is a whole another ballgame.

Be wary when a vendor claims they are using ML in their LegalTech tool or suite, and make sure to find out the specifics of what they are using ML for, and how it works.

Natural Language Processing (NLP)

It used to be that Natural Language Processing (NLP) was relatively crudely done and didn't seem impressive.

Remember those days of using NLP to try and translate a document that was in a foreign language and get it into say English?

Those used to produce some pretty hilarious translations, being quite far off of what any human translator might be able to do.

Remember those days of trying to talk to a computer system that was using NLP and the system got completely wrong the words you were saying?

Well, those days are now in the past, pretty much, and today's NLP is a lot better.

Our everyday use of Alexa and Siri are obvious examples of the use of NLP, along with a showcase of the advances in NLP.

That being said, if you use Alexa or Siri for any length of time, you very rapidly reach the edges of what the NLP can do.

It doesn't take much effort to discover the brittleness and boundaries of what NLP is able to figure out.

In a cat-and-mouse game, the AI developers and researchers that are working on NLP advancements keep improving such systems, and step-by-step those NLP capabilities are getting better.

One important aspect to keep in mind is that this NLP does not "understand" what you are saying to them.

This is something that children at first are often confused with.

Children expect that whomever they are interacting with will understand the nature of their utterances, and at first, it might seem that the NLP systems are accomplishing this, but even a child gradually realizes that the NLP isn't truly following along with what the child is expressing.

To date, we don't really know what "understanding" consists of, at least with respect to how humans understand things.

There are lots of ways to computationally model the notion of "understanding" and that's what the better NLP systems do, yet it still isn't the same as the real thing that humans seem to have.

There are a variety of aspects of NLP that are important to be aware of.

This list shows you some of the more popular and significant elements of NLP:

- Classical NLP
- ML/DL-based NLP
- Domain-Specific Modeling
- Syntax Analysis
- Tokenization
- Stemming
- Lemmatization
- Part of Speed Tagging (POST)
- Named Entity Recognition (NER)
- Dependency Parser
- Intent Analysis
- Library Use
- Open Source Use
- Proprietary
- Real-Time
- Scalability
- Etc.

One of the reasons that NLP has improved is due to the adoption of Machine Learning for the use of NLP.

Thus, there are some NLP systems that are considered classic-NLP, not making use of ML, while there are other NLP systems that are using ML.

You cannot assume that just because an NLP uses ML that it is going to be better than an NLP that doesn't use ML.

As with anything else, it all depends upon how the ML is applied to NLP.

In the use case of legal activities and LegalTech, the use of NLP is a popular AI add-on.

There are numerous software packages that provide an NLP tool or capability, thus, you don't necessarily code something from scratch to apply NLP to a particular domain, and it is relatively "easy" for a LegalTech vendor to toss NLP into their mix.

Of course, tossing something into the mix might be a good idea or a bad idea, and those that say they have NLP are sometimes doing so genuinely, while in other cases they have tried to put lipstick on a pig.

An important underpinning of any well-prepared NLP consists of its domain-related setup.

One thing that is crucial to NLP in a particular domain is loading the NLP with the domain lingo and facets.

A quick-and-dirty use of NLP doesn't go to that trouble, which generally means the NLP is not going to be very useful and convincingly accurate, while those that do earnestly make sure the domain specifics are taken into account are more likely to have a more useful NLP implementation.

Computer Vision (CV)

Computer Vision (CV) consists of having the computer system capture images and then try to ascertain what those images consist of.

CV has come a long way over the years.

This is partially due to the advances made in being able to capture images, such as better cameras and improved lenses.

This is also partially due to the advances made in computer memory capacity and speed, being able to store the images in their binary format and do so inexpensively.

This is further partially due to the speed of computer processors, along with their reduction in size, making them available at the point of the image capture, such as sitting inside a camera, rather than having to necessarily upload the image to a large-sized computer to do some kind of image processing.

One quick example of the vast improvement in CV consists of the seemingly simple act of scanning a document.

It used to be that when you scanned a document, you had a blob, and couldn't do anything with whatever text or other aspects were found in the scanned file.

Nowadays, CV is able to pretty much find and yank out the text and do the same for other sub-portions of the image. It's not perfect, and that's an important point, thus the impressive advances in CV are far from complete.

Using CV on a still image is one thing, while trying to use CV on a video stream is another.

Yes, they are similar in what they do, since you could say that a video stream is merely a whole bunch of still images, but when you try to do CV across a multitude of "still images" that are involved in video, you usually want to figure out things like where are objects moving and not moving, and other facets that involve continuity and complexities due to having associated multiple images to deal with.

There are some popular and significant aspects to be aware of about Computer Vision.

Here are some of the key facets that come up with considering the use of CV:

- Object Detection
- Scene Detection
- Facial Recognition
- Activity Detection
- Feature Extraction
- Pattern Analysis
- Still Images
- Video
- Multiple Perspectives
- Motion Estimation
- Image Reconstruction
- Labeling
- Prediction
- Analytics
- Real-Time
- Scalability
- Etc.

For legal activities and LegalTech, much of what lawyers do consists of written documents, thus the use of CV capabilities is a frequent system component.

Conclusion

There are AI technologies that you will find most frequently used in the AI add-on to LegalTech, especially Machine Learning, NLP, and Computer Vision.

I've provided some added depth for you in this chapter about those particular technologies.

The remaining AI technologies in the taxonomy are less so used for today's LegalTech, though you can expect that as LegalTech advances, there will be a further reach into the AI technologies toolkit to find more ways to enhance what LegalTech can accomplish.

Finally, it is important to note that the use of AI is often done in combination using more than one type of AI tech at a time.

For example, when trying to figure out a contract, you might first invoke a CV capability to scan a contract and take apart its inner elements.

Then, you might feed those found elements into an NLP capability.

The NLP might be using Machine Learning, doing so to figure out this contract by having ascertained various patterns from a large corpus of prior contracts.

Thus, overall, you've had to tie together Computer Vision, Natural Language Processing, and Machine Learning, neither of which alone would fully get the job done, and only in combination have a shot at being more fully useful.

———————

Note: *For supplemental materials depicting the aspects discussed in this chapter, refer to Appendix B, which contains various augmented diagrams, charts, and additional related facets of relevance.*

See Chapter 7 visuals on Figures 15-18 (pp. 195-201)

CHAPTER 8
AI AND LEGALTECH

CHAPTER 8

AI AND LEGALTECH

We've covered now the fundamentals of AI and some of the key AI technologies.

And, there has been a discussion about the nature of legal activities and LegalTech that supports and enables those legal activities.

Time to bring it all together.

There are seven (7) core AI Technologies that have been identified.

There are fifteen (15) primary legal activities that have been identified, and for which LegalTech might or might not be supporting (since some of those legal activities might be manually performed, depending upon the particular law office or practice).

Each of the core AI Technologies can be applied to each of the legal activities.

That's 7 x 15 = 105 distinct instances (yes, multiplication still works that way).

It might seem overwhelming.

That's okay, it's not so bad.

An easier way to think of the possibilities consists of writing out a somewhat simple statement to depict each of the combinations.

Here's a statement to consider:

"The use of **Machine Learning** to aid, enable, and support **Contracts** as a legal activity."

That's one of the 105 possibilities.

Essentially, take one item from column A and consider how it applies to one item from column B.

Generically, this is the same statement with the plug-ins:

"The use of **<AI Technology>** to aid, enable, and support **<Legal Activity>** as a legal activity."

The "<AI Technology> is what I'm suggesting is column A, and the "<Legal Activity" is what I'm calling as column B.

A smarmy person might ask why the statement isn't worded in the other order.

Yes, it could say this:

"The **<Legal Activity>** legal activity is aided, enabled, and supported by the use of **<AI Technology>**."

And, as an example:

"The Contracts legal activity is aided, enabled, and supported by the use of Machine Learning."

Personally, I like the former version of the order or sequence, but you are welcome to imagine them in whichever order or sequence you prefer, and there's no difference as far I'm concerned.

Proceed to consider each of the 15 such statements as they apply to Machine Learning.

- The use of **Machine Learning** to aid, enable, and support **Case Management.**

- The use of **Machine Learning** to aid, enable, and support **Contracts.**

- The use of **Machine Learning** to aid, enable, and support **Courts/Trials.**

- The use of **Machine Learning** to aid, enable, and support **Discovery.**

- The use of **Machine Learning** to aid, enable, and support **Documents/Records**.

- The use of **Machine Learning** to aid, enable, and support **IP.**

- The use of **Machine Learning** to aid, enable, and support **Law Office/Practice.**

- The use of **Machine Learning** to aid, enable, and support **Lawyer & Client Interaction**.

- The use of **Machine Learning** to aid, enable, and support **Legal Assistants.**

- The use of **Machine Learning** to aid, enable, and support **Legal Collaboration.**

- The use of **Machine Learning** to aid, enable, and support **Legal Research.**

- The use of **Machine Learning** to aid, enable, and support **Legal Workflow.**

- The use of **Machine Learning** to aid, enable, and support **Legal Writing.**

- The use of **Machine Learning** to aid, enable, and support **Professional Conduct.**

- The use of **Machine Learning** to aid, enable, and support **Other Legal Activities.**

Do the same for Knowledge-Based Systems:

- The use of **Knowledge-Based Systems** to aid, enable, and support **Case Management.**
- The use of **Knowledge-Based Systems** to aid, enable, and support **Contracts.**
- The use of **Knowledge-Based Systems** to aid, enable, and support **Courts/Trials.**
- The use of **Knowledge-Based Systems** to aid, enable, and support **Discovery.**
- The use of **Knowledge-Based Systems** to aid, enable, and support **Documents/Records.**
- The use of **Knowledge-Based Systems** to aid, enable, and support **IP.**
- The use of **Knowledge-Based Systems** to aid, enable, and support **Law Office/Practice.**
- The use of **Knowledge-Based Systems** to aid, enable, and support **Lawyer & Client Interaction.**
- The use of **Knowledge-Based Systems** to aid, enable, and support **Legal Assistants.**
- The use of **Knowledge-Based Systems** to aid, enable, and support **Legal Collaboration.**
- The use of **Knowledge-Based Systems** to aid, enable, and support **Legal Research.**
- The use of **Knowledge-Based Systems** to aid, enable, and support **Legal Workflow.**
- The use of **Knowledge-Based Systems** to aid, enable, and support **Legal Writing.**
- The use of **Knowledge-Based Systems** to aid, enable, and support **Professional Conduct.**
- The use of **Knowledge-Based Systems** to aid, enable, and support **Other Legal Activities.**

And the same for NLP:

- The use of **Natural Language Processing** to aid, enable, and support **Case Management.**

- The use of **Natural Language Processing** to aid, enable, and support **Contracts.**

- The use of **Natural Language Processing** to aid, enable, and support **Courts/Trials.**

- The use of **Natural Language Processing** to aid, enable, and support **Discovery.**

- The use of **Natural Language Processing** to aid, enable, and support **Documents/Records.**

- The use of **Natural Language Processing** to aid, enable, and support **IP.**

- The use of **Natural Language Processing** to aid, enable, and support **Law Office/Practice.**

- The use of **Natural Language Processing** to aid, enable, and support **Lawyer & Client Interaction.**

- The use of **Natural Language Processing** to aid, enable, and support **Legal Assistants.**

- The use of **Natural Language Processing** to aid, enable, and support **Legal Collaboration.**

- The use of **Natural Language Processing** to aid, enable, and support **Legal Research.**

- The use of **Natural Language Processing** to aid, enable, and support **Legal Workflow.**

- The use of **Natural Language Processing** to aid, enable, and support **Legal Writing.**

- The use of **Natural Language Processing** to aid, enable, and support **Professional Conduct.**

- The use of **Natural Language Processing** to aid, enable, and support **Other Legal Activities.**

Do the same for Computer Vision:

- The use of **Computer Vision** to aid, enable, and support **Case Management.**

- The use of **Computer Vision** to aid, enable, and support **Contracts.**

- The use of **Computer Vision** to aid, enable, and support **Courts/Trials.**

- The use of **Computer Vision** to aid, enable, and support **Discovery.**

- The use of **Computer Vision** to aid, enable, and support **Documents/Records.**

- The use of **Computer Vision** to aid, enable, and support **IP.**

- The use of **Computer Vision** to aid, enable, and support **Law Office/Practice.**

- The use of **Computer Vision** to aid, enable, and support **Lawyer & Client Interaction.**

- The use of **Computer Vision** to aid, enable, and support **Legal Assistants.**

- The use of **Computer Vision** to aid, enable, and support **Legal Collaboration.**

- The use of **Computer Vision** to aid, enable, and support **Legal Research.**

- The use of **Computer Vision** to aid, enable, and support **Legal Workflow.**

- The use of **Computer Vision** to aid, enable, and support **Legal Writing.**

- The use of **Computer Vision** to aid, enable, and support **Professional Conduct.**

- The use of **Computer Vision** to aid, enable, and support **Other Legal Activities.**

And the same for Robotics/Autonomy.

- The use of **Robotics/Autonomy** to aid, enable, and support **Case Management.**

- The use of **Robotics/Autonomy** to aid, enable, and support **Contracts.**

- The use of **Robotics/Autonomy** to aid, enable, and support **Courts/Trials.**

- The use of **Robotics/Autonomy** to aid, enable, and support **Discovery.**

- The use of **Robotics/Autonomy** to aid, enable, and support **Documents/Records.**

- The use of **Robotics/Autonomy** to aid, enable, and support **IP.**

- The use of **Robotics/Autonomy** to aid, enable, and support **Law Office/Practice.**

- The use of **Robotics/Autonomy** to aid, enable, and support **Lawyer & Client Interaction.**

- The use of **Robotics/Autonomy** to aid, enable, and support **Legal Assistants.**

- The use of **Robotics/Autonomy** to aid, enable, and support **Legal Collaboration.**

- The use of **Robotics/Autonomy** to aid, enable, and support **Legal Research.**

- The use of **Robotics/Autonomy** to aid, enable, and support **Legal Workflow.**

- The use of **Robotics/Autonomy** to aid, enable, and support **Legal Writing.**

- The use of **Robotics/Autonomy** to aid, enable, and support **Professional Conduct.**

- The use of **Robotics/Autonomy** to aid, enable, and support **Other Legal Activities.**

Do the same for Common-Sense Reasoning:

- The use of **Common-Sense Reasoning** to aid, enable, and support **Case Management.**
- The use of **Common-Sense Reasoning** to aid, enable, and support **Contracts.**
- The use of **Common-Sense Reasoning** to aid, enable, and support **Courts/Trials.**
- The use of **Common-Sense Reasoning** to aid, enable, and support **Discovery.**
- The use of **Common-Sense Reasoning** to aid, enable, and support **Documents/Records.**
- The use of **Common-Sense Reasoning** to aid, enable, and support **IP.**
- The use of **Common-Sense Reasoning** to aid, enable, and support **Law Office/Practice.**
- The use of **Common-Sense Reasoning** to aid, enable, and support **Lawyer & Client Interaction.**
- The use of **Common-Sense Reasoning** to aid, enable, and support **Legal Assistants.**
- The use of **Common-Sense Reasoning** to aid, enable, and support **Legal Collaboration.**
- The use of **Common-Sense Reasoning** to aid, enable, and support **Legal Research.**
- The use of **Common-Sense Reasoning** to aid, enable, and support **Legal Workflow.**
- The use of **Common-Sense Reasoning** to aid, enable, and support **Legal Writing.**
- The use of **Common-Sense Reasoning** to aid, enable, and support **Professional Conduct.**
- The use of **Common-Sense Reasoning** to aid, enable, and support **Other Legal Activities.**

And, finally, the same for Other AI Technologies.

- The use of **Other AI Technologies** to aid, enable, and support **Case Management**.

- The use of **Other AI Technologies** to aid, enable, and support **Contracts**.

- The use of **Other AI Technologies** to aid, enable, and support **Courts/Trials**.

- The use of **Other AI Technologies** to aid, enable, and support **Discovery**.

- The use of **Other AI Technologies** to aid, enable, and support **Documents/Records**.

- The use of **Other AI Technologies** to aid, enable, and support **IP**.

- The use of **Other AI Technologies** to aid, enable, and support **Law Office/Practice**.

- The use of **Other AI Technologies** to aid, enable, and support **Lawyer & Client Interaction**.

- The use of **Other AI Technologies** to aid, enable, and support **Legal Assistants**.

- The use of **Other AI Technologies** to aid, enable, and support **Legal Collaboration**.

- The use of **Other AI Technologies** to aid, enable, and support **Legal Research**.

- The use of **Other AI Technologies** to aid, enable, and support **Legal Workflow**.

- The use of **Other AI Technologies** to aid, enable, and support **Legal Writing**.

- The use of **Other AI Technologies** to aid, enable, and support **Professional Conduct**.

- The use of **Other AI Technologies** to aid, enable, and support **Other Legal Activities**.

Whew, that was exhausting.

There must be a better way to think about this.

Voila, there is.

A matrix can be used to depict the matter.

For the rows, we'll use the various AI Technologies.

Thus, seven rows.

For the columns, we'll use the various legal activities.

Thus, fifteen columns.

You now have a very handy matrix that can be used for very handy purposes.

One purpose would be to figure out for any LegalTech vendor that has an offering software of one kind or another, which columns they cover.

In other words, which of the legal activities does their system or tool purport to cover?

Once you've got that figured, the next aspect would be which of those such columns are making use of AI in some manner.

You could put X's or some marking inside the matrix cells to indicate which of the legal activities (per columns) are using which of the AI Technologies (per the rows).

For those of you that think the columns ought to be the AI Technologies and the rows ought to be the Legal Activities, sure, let's do that too.

The matrix can be shown as fifteen rows (legal activities) by seven columns (AI Technologies).

Choose whichever matrix version is best suited to whatever use you have in mind.

For each, their own cup of tea.

Scoring Is Good

I mentioned that you could put an "X" or some other mark into the cells, denoting when there is a purported match of a legal activity being supported or enabled via an AI technology.

That could be useful, though having something other than a simple mark might be even more useful.

For example, you might want to score or rate how well the AI technology is being applied to a particular legal activity.

I like to use a straightforward metric.

Let's use a numeric score of zero to five.

A score of zero means that the AI isn't being applied to the legal activity.

This could be because the vendor hasn't attempted to do so, or it could also be that they have tried to do so but it is utterly ineffective and incomplete, therefore, you opted to give a zero.

A score of 1 means that the AI is slimly applied.

And so on, using this scoring:

    0 = None

    1 = Slim

    2 = Some

    3 = Modest

    4 = Much

    5 = Full

Is this metric a completely cut-and-dry measurement?

Nope.

To some degree, it is based on expert judgment about the degree to which the AI technology is being applied.

You can quantify it somewhat, by establishing a set of criteria and adding points and weights, though this is something only usually done when you have a higher burden of "proof" about why the scores have come out the way they did.

Likewise, some might not like the word choices associated with the numeric scores.

What does it mean to say that something is "modest" as per its application of AI versus something that is "slim" as applied to AI?

I used words that seem to generally provide an overall impression, and you are welcome to use some other wording that you believe might be better for your circumstance at hand.

Conclusion

Applying AI to the various legal activities is something that the industry is trying mightily to do.

If you were to use the matrix approach and fill-in for all of the existing LegalTech products as to how many have an AI component, the resulting matrix would be rather sparse.

That's good, since it provides lots of opportunities, and I'll be exploring those opportunities in a later chapter.

That's bad, meaning that if you are desirous of having off-the-shelf LegalTech that's using AI and ready-to-go, your pickings are currently rather slim (see, the word "slim" is quite handy!).

In the future, we'll have a lot more of these aspects being covered.

Speaking of the future, this brings up another one of those chicken-or-the-egg conundrums.

Some argue that when I refer to AI and LegalTech, it is odd since AI is being singled out.

In their view, AI should be considered wholly within LegalTech, thus, it makes no sense to say "AI and" when it is really that AI is found within the rubric of LegalTech itself.

I get the point, thanks, and sympathize with their argument.

I agree that it is ultimately going to be the case that AI is within LegalTech and you will fully expect AI to be used in there.

Perhaps the AI will be so commonly used that it won't even stick out and won't be a competitive differentiator of one offering of LegalTech versus another.

Looking forward to that day!

We aren't there as yet.

Therefore, I am willing to separately call out that there is something known as AI and LegalTech, which is to-date rather uncommon and only slowly taking hold.

Note: *For supplemental materials depicting the aspects discussed in this chapter, refer to Appendix B, which contains various augmented diagrams, charts, and additional related facets of relevance.*

See Chapter 8 visuals on Figures 19 – 31 (pp. 203-227)

CHAPTER 9
CASE STUDY:
CONTRACTXPERT

CHAPTER 9

CASE STUDY: CONTRACTXPERT

We've covered the fundamentals of AI and discussed how AI tech can be applied to a range of legal activities, preferably already being digitally undertaken via LegalTech.

Let's put the framework to use via a case study.

There's a company that I'll refer to as the Widget Company (real name to be unstated to protect the innocent and the guilty).

They have a nifty software package known as "ContractXpert" (this is a made-up name, and so if it resembles any actual named product it is not the same product and any semblance is unrelated).

You are interested in their software because it claims to be a better way to deal with legal contracts.

Who wouldn't want that?

As a lawyer, you'd welcome something that could make your life easier when drafting and reviewing contracts.

A law firm or practice would welcome something that could make the drafting and review of contracts easier and less prone to having any overlooked omissions or contain errors, handy across-the-board for the entire firm.

As a researcher, you'd like to know how AI is being applied to the law and so this notion of having a souped-up contracts analyzer seems interesting.

As a competitor, it would be useful to know what other firms are providing to the marketplace.

So, for whatever reason, you take a look at the online brochure of ContractXpert at the Widget Company website, and here's what you see:

1. **"Our AI identifies for you numerous contract elements including text, tables, headings**

2. **Allows for ease of contract searches by your legal team**

3. **Creates a semantic understanding of contract obligations, parties, rights**

4. **Can be used to compare multiple contracts**

5. **Deal with contracts faster and more reliably"**

Sounds attractive.

Right away, the claim by the vendor is that their software includes AI (per the brochure it clearly states in the first bullet point that "Our AI identifies...").

Sensational!

Some vendors might not tout their AI use, though since it is a potential competitive differentiator, you would anticipate that most vendors will proudly say they are using AI, which the Widget Company is happy to do.

In this case, the vendor claims they are using AI.

Normally, a non-AI versed person would accept blindly that AI is indeed being used.

And perhaps be (unduly) impressed.

Not those of you reading this book

You now know better!

Hopefully, your mind is already racing with questions such as what type of AI is being used, what does it do, how does it work, what good is it, etc.

Let's see what we can tease further out of the brochure's bullet points.

The first bullet point claims that the "AI identifies for you numerous contract elements including text, tables, headings."

This is reminiscent of how Computer Vision can be used to detect text and images within a scanned-in document.

From the bullet point, we can't yet discern whether the ContractXpert is going to examine blob-like scanned documents, or whether it expects a document to be in normal text format, to begin with.

We'd want to get that facet clarified.

Either way, it does seem useful to be able to have the software identify various "objects" within the document and be able to presumably readily pull them out or find them.

At this juncture or our review, though, it does seem rather simplistic and not going to be overly helpful.

If that's the only use of AI, it would seem rather marginal.

For example, we can't discern whether the computer will be able to do anything with the elements, and might only be able to proffer those elements, which could be handy but not as much as we'd expect for the use of AI.

Let's read further.

The second bullet point says that the software will allow you to readily do contract searches.

Yes, though to what degree does the search act in a "smart" way and have any kind of realization about the elements within the contracts?

Doesn't seem to give us a warm and fuzzy feeling about the embracing of AI in their product.

In the third bullet, the vendor says that a semantic understanding of contract obligations, parties, rights are the capability of the ContractXpert.

Now it's getting closer to something we can feel more comfortable labeling as AI.

Natural Language Processing (NLP) tries to create semantic relationships between things, doing so to be able to "understand" language that is being used.

We'd need to find out more how the ContractXpert sets up the semantic relationships and what they accomplish.

Questions that would come to mind include:

- Is it able to properly find all contract obligations or are some potentially missed?

- Is it able to properly identify all parties of the contract or are some potentially misclassified or missed?

- Is it able to detect the rights being embodied, or does it miss some or misstate some?

- Etc.

The fourth bullet point indicates that multiple contracts can be compared.

Certainly, a useful feature.

One wonders if they are able to compare multiple contracts, have they considered using Machine Learning, doing so to identify patterns across contracts and be able to possibly aid the creation or review of new contracts?

This comes to mind since if they have the capability to deal with multiple contracts it implies data, possibly lots of data, collected across a corpus of contracts.

Maybe.

The bullet doesn't mention anything about ML.

Probably either due to the aspect that they aren't using ML, or might be they don't even know anything about ML and how it could be useful to their product (they might have a bent toward CV and NLP, and not be familiar with ML).

Finally, the last bullet point indicates that the ContractXpert allows you to deal with contracts faster and more reliably.

Of course, it's vital to know why any use of AI is going to be a payoff, though we would want to find out how it is that the claim of dealing with contracts on a faster basis and reliably is being touted.

Do they have existing customers that can attest to this productivity claim?

Or, what do they have to validate the claim?

Well, that's our initial analysis based on the brochure info.

There's enough there to warrant taking a closer look.

Shift ahead in time and imagine that we were able to get access to the ContractXpert on a demo basis and were able to speak with a rep that could answer our questions about the software package.

Time to rate the software.

After digging into things, they turned out to be using some ML.

They didn't mention it in the brochure because it was only marginally being used, though it is on their internal list of future expansions related to the product.

We'll give them a 1 or a rating of "slim" for ML.

Admittedly, that's a tad generous, and especially since they don't mention it themselves, but they appear to be on the ML path and so giving them some recognition for it seems reasonable.

In terms of the finding of elements in a document such as text, tables, and so on, they aren't doing so on a purely scanned blob, and instead expect the source document to be already in normal text format.

Thus, let's give their use of CV a zero since they aren't using it.

The source document detection is being done by NLP, and that's also what does the semantic relationship effort.

After trying various sample contracts, the NLP is doing not as much as one might have hoped for, and so I'll be (again) generous and give a score of 3 for "modest" use of NLP (when I mentioned this to the rep, this angered the rep, he claimed they ought to be a 5 or "full" score; sorry, not on my watch).

They aren't using any other AI tech and so the other categories all get a zero.

Next, let's carry the scoring over into the big picture matrix.

The Widget Company is a small business startup and their only offering is ContractXpert.

Thus, in the matrix of AI tech versus legal activities, the only column relevant to them is the one about contracts.

If you'd like to have the rows be the legal activities and the columns are the AI tech, you could arrange the matrix that way instead.

Upon reviewing the results of having looked closely at ContractXpert, here's a bottom-line recap:

- Very simplistic and mainly off-the-shelf NLP

- Doesn't leverage ML

- Semantic extraction at times off-target

- No built-in error detection/correction

- Lacks any semblance of "legal reasoning"

- Slight step-up on typical e-contracts features

- Provides promise if further advanced

- Need to do cost/benefit to ascertain value

- Claims of contracts faster/reliable TBD

Conclusion

The rep pointed out to me that their product is better than most other e-contract offerings.

That's a fair point (though not yet substantiated).

This review was more done about how far or advanced the capability made use of AI in an absolute sense, rather than on a relative basis in comparison to other industry offerings.

Anyway, this hopefully gives you a sense of how to make use of the AI LegalTech tools and background that's been provided in this book.

———

Note: *For supplemental materials depicting the aspects discussed in this chapter, refer to Appendix B, which contains various augmented diagrams, charts, and additional related facets of relevance.*

See Chapter 9 visuals on Figures 32-36 (pp. 229-237)

CHAPTER 10
OPPORTUNITIES FOR
AI LEGALTECH

CHAPTER 10

OPPORTUNITIES FOR
AI LEGALTECH

The sky is the limit.

That's the way to think about the opportunities for AI being applied to legal activities and LegalTech.

If you were to ask me about FinTech (financially oriented tech), I'd say that there's a lot of AI-related add-ons and integrations already in the FinTech niche. This doesn't mean that you'd be misguided to aim for FinTech, but it would be a field that you'd want to be quite mindful and wary about doing something that someone else has already done.

The nice thing about LegalTech is that the odds are pretty good that whatever you do with AI, there are few others that have done much in the same way, or even at all.

Nearly a clean slate.

That's a dual-edged sword.

Getting lawyers and law firms to be willing to make use of AI-enabled LegalTech is not going to be especially easy.

Besides the stubbornness of often clinging to what was good enough before, and being innately leery of using tech, the cost to acquire or license AI add-ons is another tough hurdle.

Generally, law offices are known for being tightwads.

Some might consider that an insult (i.e., being called a tightwad or penny pincher), while others would point out with pride that it illustrates how careful they are about their spending.

The size of the market is another factor.

According to Statista Research, the United States spends about $3 billion on legal software annually.

That's a decent-sized market, plus it doesn't even include the rest of the world's expenditures on legal software, yet it still isn't a massive sized market per se.

Anyway, as mentioned in the earlier chapters, there are lots of pressures and reasons for lawyers and law practices to reconsider their resistance to getting new tech.

The compounded annual growth rate (CAGR) for AI LegalTech is predicted to be around 36% over the next six years (per Statista Research).

There are going to be opportunities.

Perhaps for you!

Startups in LegalTech are already hot, and those with AI and LegalTech are getting special attention.

Okay, how can you figure out what opportunity is good for you?

There are two ways to potentially proceed (well, there are more than two, but these are two that I'm recommending here).

1. **Start with a legal activity and then explore the AI side of things, or**

2. **Start with an AI tech and then explore the legal activity side of things**

I'll start with the version of my recommended steps that involves you already knowing something about legal activities and the law, and not especially having to know much about AI (other than having read this introductory book).

Do so as though you are willing to think outside-the-box.

Pick a legal activity that you know well.

Recall, here's the list:
- Case Management
- Contracts
- Courts/Trials
- Discovery
- Documents/Records
- IP
- Law Office/Practice
- Lawyer & Client Interaction
- Legal Assistants
- Legal Collaboration
- Legal Research
- Legal Workflow
- Legal Writing
- Professional Conduct
- Other

This makes sense to pick one that you know because you'll be able to use that as your initial grounding and feel confident in doing so.

Also, I usually recommend you pick one, rather than several, and see how it goes with each one separately, doing so one-at-at-time (don't bite off more than you can chew).

Next, take a look at each of the AI Technologies that have been discussed herein.

Recall, these are the AI Technologies mentioned:
- Machine Learning (ML)
- Knowledge-Based Systems (KBS)
- Natural Language Processing (NLP)
- Computer Vision (CV)
- Robotics / Autonomy
- Common-Sense Reasoning
- Other Technologies

For each one of the AI Technologies, try to imagine how the legal activity that you already know well might be changed via adopting that particular AI technology.

Ask yourself some crucial questions.

Would the adoption of that AI allow you to perform that legal activity faster, or easier, or with fewer errors, or in ways that there would be a demonstrative payoff or benefit to adding the AI?

If your answer is yes, you should next dig more deeply, while if your answer is no, then you should probably look at the list of legal activities again and find a different one on the list to explore (proceed as such).

And, if you ultimately go through all of them on the list, and none seem suitable, something has gone awry, and I think that you are somehow veering from what I've been trying to advise and might need to relook back at some of the chapters (thus, I'm going to assume that this "exhaustive" outcome won't happen).

Okay, you should have one legal activity that you've got in mind and that you've toyed with in terms of how AI might make a substantive difference.

Learn more about that AI technology so that you can become more versed in what it could do and how it could be applied to that legal activity.

You are ready to then research what's in the marketplace.

Do some online searching to find companies that are already doing something akin to what you have in mind.

Similar to the case study about ContractXpert, try to figure out whether your notion is merely the same, or whether you might have something that's unique or not yet well-implemented.

Keep in mind too that there's the big issue of whether there is LegalTech already that will provide the needed digital foundation, or whether you'll need to start from scratch to get the legal activity into a digital usable condition.

If there isn't any kind of LegalTech as the base, it's going to be a steeper uphill climb.

By this point in your exploration, you'd likely be ready to start putting together a business plan about how you might further proceed.

In today's world of startups, please be aware and forewarned that most are eschewing a "business plan" so don't call it that.

Part of the reason that "business plan" has gone out the window is that many used to make the plan itself overtake everything else.

Analysis paralysis would sink in.

The time and resources it took to craft a business plan were overshadowing the timing of grasping a fleeting and open window of opportunity.

Unfortunately, the baby was thrown out with the bathwater and the very existence and idea of business plans were considered toxic and never to be undertaken.

The reality is that everyone ultimately does some kind of "business plan" and yet they can't refer to it in that way, else they'll be considered backward and outdated in their methods.

My point is that you should put together a business plan, just call it something else, such as that it is your "roadmap" or that it is your "startup deck" or anything else that's hip and in vogue.

I'll cover a bit more about how to prepare that roadmap in a moment.

First, though, remember that I said there were two paths to go on how to initially proceed.

I'd like to quote myself, if I may:

"There are two ways to potentially proceed (well, there are more than two, but these are two that I'm recommending here).
1. Start with a legal activity and then explore the AI side of things, or
2. Start with an AI tech and then explore the legal activity side of things"

Wise words!

I've covered the first approach.

What about the second approach?

The second approach is quite similar to the first approach, just follow the same steps I've already outlined, though you are beginning with the AI and trying to find a suitable match to a legal activity.

In a sense, the second approach isn't usually as advisable.

The reason for not especially taking the second approach is that it assumes that you are versed in AI and are hopeful of finding something in the target domain to apply AI to.

That's fine, it just is difficult if you don't know much or anything about the domain being targeted.

This is a long-time and unresolved argument about which way is the best to go.

Do you have in-hand some nifty AI tech that you go around trying to find ways to apply it?

That's the solution looking for a problem, some say.

Or, you do find a problem, such as a legal activity that could be done in a better way, and then find a solution that will solve that problem.

Obviously, if you know AI and don't know about legal activities, you pretty much are going to start with the AI for this pin the tail on the donkey exercise.

If you don't especially know AI, but you do know about legal activities, you are most likely better off to start with what you know, the legal activities, and proceed from there.

Oftentimes, you'll see a pairing that happens when these kinds of opportunity brainstorming discussions or workshops take place.

One person knows about the law and legal activities, and the other knows about AI and tech.

They join together and thus can have two minds for the price of one.

Well, in that case, I'll say this to the AI person, keep your eye on the member of your pairing that knows the law and be careful that they don't try to pull the wool over your eyes about who is going to own what rights to whatever you come up with.

If that seems callous, I apologize.

Meanwhile, if you are the law and legal activities person of the pairing, watch out for the AI person that has their own favored AI crush and they are gushing about it, and unwilling to consider any downsides, since they could readily lead you down a primrose path that won't end very well.

If that seems callous, I apologize (once again).

The overall point is that when you pair up, please do so with your eyes wide open.

I've stated that you should consider one legal activity at a time.

That's the easiest way to get started with the exercise in finding opportunities.

Rather than a standalone or singular choice, it might make sense to look at several at the same time.

There are LegalTech suites that contain a multitude of apps or components.

The question then arises whether any of those apps are ripe for adding AI, and if so, which ones, and in which sequence would it make the most sense to do so.

.

Suppose there was a LegalTech suite that covered seven of the fifteen kinds of legal activities.

Imagine further that AI is already being used with the suite.

You could use the matrices that we've previously discussed to map out where the coverage is, along with whether it is sufficient, etc.

Conclusion

There are lots of opportunities in AI and LegalTech.

For those of you that are contemplating putting together a startup in the realm of AI and LegalTech, I applaud you.

I'll also mention that it is likely to be a rocky road.

Don't let that discourage you!

Anyway, for any startup, you ought to be thinking about all of the various parts and pieces that you'll need to put together.

For your convenience, I'll list the key elements of any startup, a subject that I've covered in-depth in one of my other books, and has successfully been used by numerous startups across all fields and all areas of tech.

For the details, please refer to my other book.

Take a look on the next page at the listing of key elements.

In any case, the key startup elements are:

1. Solvable problem

2. Viable solution

3. The customers

4. This similar to

5. Core business model

6. Product/service

7. Differentiation

8. Startup funding

9. Monetization

10. Unfair advantage

11. About the presenter (when doing a pitch)

12. About the team

13. Accomplished to-date

14. The ask

15. Cost structure

16. Exit strategy

17. Marketing

18. The competition

19. Prior pitches (when pitching)

20. The pitch (your deck or business plan)

I'm not going to cover those herein, but point them out to let you know that putting together a proper roadmap (business plan!) is more than scrawling something on the back of a napkin (you can do that to get going, but it's not something that most investors are going to providing much funding for).

I will though help you get started with the plan.

Item number 6 is where you state the product or service of your startup-.

If you've done what I have suggested in this chapter and figured out a potential candidate legal activity and one or more AI technologies that will aid it, you've done your initial homework for item number 6, congratulations.

You are already one-twentieth of the way there on doing your roadmap!

Note: *For supplemental materials depicting the aspects discussed in this chapter, refer to Appendix B, which contains various augmented diagrams, charts, and additional related facets of relevance.*

See Chapter 10 visuals on Figures 37-41 (pp. 239-247)

CHAPTER 11
KEEPING UP WITH AI LEGALTECH

CHAPTER 11

KEEPING UP WITH
AI LEGALTECH

In this chapter, I've put together a collection of useful resources for you to consider perusing as part of an ongoing effort to keep up with what's happening in the field of AI and the law, especially regarding the LegalTech side of things.

I include an indication of what the resource is about, along with providing links for you to then follow-up to get additional information about each such resource.

It is my hope that you will indeed do a follow-up and continue what you've started to do, namely, become a contributor in one means or another in the emerging, exciting, and expanding field of AI and the law.

This call to contribute to the field applies to everyone, including whether you are or are intending to become a lawyer, an entrepreneur, a researcher, a scholar, a teacher, an executive, a vendor, or in whatever capacity you might proceed.

My compilation includes these resource indications:
- **Stanford University Resources**
- **Articles On LegalTech Courses In Law Schools**
- **Annual Conferences on LegalTech**
- **Law-Related Tech Journals**
- **Top AI Journals**
- **Close-up Look At Some AI LegalTech Products**

Stanford University Resources

One especially important resource for you to use in your quest would be to take a look at the Stanford Center for Legal Informatics.

Stanford has established CodeX, the Stanford Center for Legal Informatics, which serves this stated purpose:

"At CodeX, researchers, lawyers, entrepreneurs and technologists work side-by-side to advance the frontier of legal technology, bringing new levels of legal efficiency, transparency, and access to legal systems around the world. CodeX's emphasis is on the research and development of computational law — the branch of legal informatics concerned with the automation and mechanization of legal analysis."

Source: https://law.stanford.edu/codex-the-stanford-center-for-legal-informatics/

You'll find that CodeX has a quite impressive array of projects, blogs, events, courses, publications, social media, and other aspects, so make sure to take a look at https://law.stanford.edu/codex-the-stanford-center-for-legal-informatics/

Dr. Roland Vogl is Executive Director of CodeX and Executive Director of the Stanford Program in Law, Science, and Technology.

The Research Director is Dr. Michael Genesereth, Associate Professor of Computer Science and Associate Professor, by courtesy, of Law, and Research Director for CodeX.

An excellent paper that you might want to read is by Dr. Michael Genesereth in which he provides crucial insights into the field of Computational Law, the piece is entitled "Computational Law: The Cop In The Backseat."

Here's the abstract:

"Computational Law is that branch of legal informatics concerned with the mechanization of legal analysis (whether done by humans or machines). It emphasizes explicit behavioral constraints and eschews implicit rules of conduct. Importantly, there is a commitment to a level of rigor in specifying laws that is sufficient to support entirely mechanical processing. While the idea of mechanized legal analysis is not new, its prospects are better than ever due to recent technological developments – including progress in Computational Logic, the growth of the Internet, and the proliferation of autonomous systems (such as self-driving cars and robots). Legal technology based on Computational Law has the potential to dramatically change the legal profession, improving the quality and efficiency of legal services and possibly disrupting the way law firms do business. More broadly, the technology has the potential to bring legal understanding and legal tools to everyone in society, not just legal professionals, thus enhancing access to justice and improving the legal system as a whole."

Source:
http://logic.stanford.edu/publications/genesereth/complaw.pdf

You might also want to consider taking a look at the Stanford Law & Policy Review journal.

There's an interesting recent article in the Stanford Law & Policy Review journal that covers facets of AI, written by Karni A. Chagal-Feferkorn and the piece is entitled "Am I an Algorithm or a Product? When Products Liability Should Apply to Algorithmic Decision-Makers" (Volume 30, Issue 1, 2019).

The description of the article is:

"This Article proposes a new approach for distinguishing traditional products from "thinking algorithms" for the purpose of determining whether products liability should apply. Instead of examining the system's characteristics in isolation, I propose a "purposive interpretation" approach: one that analyzes the system's characteristics vis-à-vis the rationales behind the products liability legal framework, and identifies those associated with promoting said rationales versus ones adversely affecting the ability to accomplish them. The Article will thus offer a novel, practical method for differentiating traditional products from thinking algorithms, based on fulfilling the rationales behind products liability laws and hence provide decision-makers with tools to better decide when products liability should apply and when it should not."

Source: https://law.stanford.edu/publications/am-i-an-algorithm-or-a-product-when-products-liability-should-apply-to-algorithmic-decision-makers/

In case you aren't familiar with the Stanford Law & Policy Review, here's some helpful background info:

"Stanford Law & Policy Review (SLPR) is one of the most prominent policy journals in the nation and informs public discourse by publishing articles that analyze the intersection of our legal system with local, state, and federal policy. SLPR is ideologically neutral and solicits articles from authors who represent a diversity of political viewpoints. Founded in 1989 by Stanford Law School students, SLPR has long been a forum not only for academics but also for high-profile policymakers to publish articles on hot-button issues."

Source: https://law.stanford.edu/Harvard-law-policy-review-slpr/

Articles On LegalTech Courses In Law Schools

Law schools are gradually offering courses in LegalTech, and hopefully will also be including the topic of AI, though just getting any LegalTech coverage is a welcome advancement for many such training grounds of budding lawyers.

Here's a recent depiction of how such a LegalTech course might be undertaken, as described in the Computer Law & Security Review, April 2020, Volume 36, in an article entitled "A Call For Introducing LegalTech In The Classroom" by Chris Ireland and Ryan Hockley:

Per the article summary:

"Change is coming to the way the business of law is conducted. It is an unavoidable reality that the delivery of professional legal services is on the cusp of major disruption. The way law firms, and in-house legal teams operate is predicted to change dramatically. It is that a majority of the aforementioned change will come from the adoption of more sophisticated technology by law firms and the courts. Technological change has already made some lawyer hours obsolete, and this trend is only expected to continue. Given this incoming wave of change, there exists a strong justification for the inclusion of legaltech in the undergraduate LLB curriculum. This article assesses the feasibility of such an inclusion and provides suggestions for what institutions could be doing to support their users."

Source:
https://www.sciencedirect.com/science/article/pii/S0267364920300042

One law and tech publication that I regularly read is the Santa Clara High Technology Law Journal, which describes itself this way:

"The Santa Clara High Technology Law Journal (HTLJ) is a scholarly publication of the Santa Clara University School of Law. HTLJ is a leading forum for multidisciplinary discourse on emerging issues at the intersection of technology, law, and public policy. Prior to Volume 30, the journal was known as the Computer and High Technology Law Journal."

Source: https://law.scu.edu/high-tech-law-journal/

It has been around since the mid-1980s and has more recently made its articles available for free via the Digital Commons platform: https://digitalcommons.law.scu.edu/chtlj/

There's a recent article about the role of tech education for law students, explored in an article entitled "A Perspective On Technology Education For Law Students" by Anthony Volini, February 2020, Volume 36, Issue 2, and the article describes itself this way:

"Law schools continue to appreciate the importance of technology awareness for law students practicing in the 21st Century. As law schools have a desire to educate law students on technology, there is a need for focusing curricular priorities in this relatively new endeavor. The need for technology education in law schools is especially urgent, considering so many statutes either directly or indirectly require cybersecurity controls, and lawyers without a foundation in technology struggle to advise on such matters. This essay thus proposes curricular priorities to help law students face the challenges of an increasingly tech-driven legal marketplace and enable them to improve on bridging the communication gap between lawyers and technologists. This essay analogizes learning technology to learning a second language (e.g., Spanish) as a way to conceptualize tech education for law students with no tech background. Conceptually, law schools can enable students to achieve an intermediate level of tech fluency to facilitate further learning outside of law school."

Source: https://digitalcommons.law.scu.edu/chtlj/vol36/iss2/2/

In the Harvard Journal of Law & Technology, you might find this article of interest, entitled "A Primer On Using Artificial Intelligence In The Legal Profession," published on January 03, 2018, and was authored by Lauri Donahue, which per the article indicates:

"Lauri Donahue is a 1986 graduate of Harvard Law School and was one of the co-founders of the Harvard Journal of Law & Technology. She is now the Director of Legal Content for LawGeex, a Tel Aviv legaltech startup."

It's a relatively short piece and provides a quick overview of AI facets and some indications about the legal profession.

Here's what the article says about the potential impact of AI:

"According to Deloitte, about 100,000 legal sector jobs are likely to be automated in the next twenty years. Deloitte claims 39% of legal jobs can be automated; McKinsey Global Institute estimates that 23% of a lawyer's job could be automated. Some estimates suggest that adopting all legal technology (including AI) already available now would reduce lawyers' hours by 13%."

Source: https://jolt.law.harvard.edu/digest/a-primer-on-using-artificial-intelligence-in-the-legal-profession

In case you aren't familiar with the Harvard Journal of Law & Technology, here's a description about it:

"The Harvard Journal of Law & Technology is a biannual open access law journal, established at Harvard Law School in 1988. It covers all aspects of technology law, including intellectual property, biotechnology, privacy law, computer law, cybercrime, antitrust, space law, telecommunications, the Internet, and e-commerce."

Source: https://jolt.law.harvard.edu/

Annual Conferences On LegalTech

One conference known for its focus on LegalTech occurs annually in New York City.

Here's what their website says about the event:

"Legaltech is the largest and most important legal technology event of the year. Legaltech provides an in-depth look at what the technological world has in store for you and your practice AND offers an expansive exhibit floor with the most extensive gathering of innovative products designed to meet your current and future technology needs."

Source: https://www.event.law.com/legaltech

Exhibitors in the AI Category include:
- Agiloft
- ayfie
- BILR
- BlackBerry
- Blue J Legal
- Casepoint
- Cellebrite
- ContractPodAi
- ContractRoom
- DISCO
- eBrevia
- EDT Software
- Epiq
- Everchron
- Evisort
- Exterro

- Global Relay Communications
- iConect Development
- Iconic Translation Machines
- ikaun
- iManage
- Ipro Tech
- Iristel
- KLDiscovery
- KL Software Technologies
- Knovos
- Knowable
- Legal Suite
- Lextrado
- Lionbridge Legal
- Mutual Mobile
- NetDocuments
- NetGovern
- Nexidia
- Now Discovery
- Nuix
- OpenText
- Relativity
- Reveal Data
- Rippe & Kingston Solutions
- SDL
- Servient
- ThoughtTrace
- TransPerfect Legal Solutions
- Veritone
- Vertical Discovery
- Wolters Kluwer ELM Solutions

Law-Related Tech Journals

There are a number of highly regarded law-related tech journals that provide coverage generally about technology and the law, and occasionally include a smattering of AI aspects (though not very often, regrettably, and certainly not as often as I'd like).

In any case, here's a listing based on a ranking by Google Scholar, showing the Top 20 technology law journals. Don't be fixated by the ranking, which is based on a formula involving the number of articles and the citations and other facets.

Just think of this list as the Top 20 and numbered for ease of reference rather than importance or priority per se:

1. Computer Law & Security Review
2. Berkeley Technology Law Journal
3. International Data Privacy Law
4. Minnesota Journal of Law, Science & Technology
5. Vanderbilt Journal of Entertainment and Technology Law
6. World Patent Information
7. Pharmaceutical Patent Analyst
8. IIC-International Review of Intellectual Property and Competition Law
9. Journal on Telecommunications & High Technology Law
10. Columbia Journal of Law & the Arts
11. International Review of Law, Computers & Technology
12. European Data Protection Law Review
13. Journal of Intellectual Property Law & Practice
14. John Marshall Review of Intellectual Property Law
15. Journal of Intellectual Property, Information Technology & Electronic Communication Law
16. Federal Communications Law Journal
17. Journal of Intellectual Property
18. Journal of the Patent and Trademark Office Society
19. Journal of Antitrust Enforcement
20. Journal of European Consumer and Market Law

Source:
https://scholar.google.com/citations?view_op=top_venues&hl=en&vq=eng_technologylaw

Top AI Journals

Here's a ranking of the Top 50 AI journals, according to their SJR rating.

As background:

"The SCImago Journal & Country Rank is a publicly available portal that includes the journals and country scientific indicators developed from the information contained in the Scopus® database. These indicators can be used to assess and analyze scientific domains. Journals can be compared or analysed separately."

"This platform takes its name from the SCImago Journal Rank (SJR) indicator (PDF), developed by SCImago from the widely known algorithm Google PageRank™."

Source:
https://www.scimagojr.com/journalrank.php?category=1702&year=2015

1. IEEE Transactions on Pattern Analysis and Machine Intelligence
2. Foundations and Trends in Machine Learning
3. IEEE Transactions on Fuzzy Systems
4. International Journal of Computer Vision
5. Journal of Memory and Language
6. Cognitive Psychology
7. International Journal of Robotics Research
8. Soft Robotics
9. IEEE Transactions on Neural Networks and Learning Systems
10. Physics of Life Reviews
11. Journal of the ACM
12. Fuzzy Optimization and Decision Making
13. Information Sciences
14. Cognitive Science
15. Autonomous Robots

16. International Journal of Approximate Reasoning
17. Knowledge-Based Systems
18. Artificial Intelligence
19. Topics in Cognitive Science
20. IEEE Transactions on Human-Machine Systems
21. Pattern Recognition
22. Expert Systems with Applications
23. 2012 2nd International Conference on Applied Robotics for the Power Industry, CARPI 2012
24. Journal of Semantics
25. Journal of Machine Learning Research
26. Neural Networks
27. Networks and Spatial Economics
28. Journal of Automated Reasoning
29. Fuzzy Sets and Systems
30. Systems Science and Control Engineering
31. ACM Transactions on Intelligent Systems and Technology
32. Machine Learning
33. Journal of Intelligent Manufacturing
34. Design Studies
35. International Journal of Intelligent Systems
36. Journal of Pragmatics
37. 31st International Conference on Machine Learning, ICML 2014
38. Theory and Practice of Logic Programming
39. Swarm Intelligence
40. Journal of Artificial Intelligence Research
41. Argument and Computation
42. Engineering Applications of Artificial Intelligence
43. Proceedings – IEEE International Conference on Robotics and Automation
44. Journal of Heuristics
45. Advanced Engineering Informatics
46. Neurocomputing
47. International Journal of Artificial Intelligence
48. Pattern Recognition Letters
49. Frontiers in Neurorobotics
50. Integrated Computer-Aided Engineering

Close-up Look At Some AI LegalTech Products

I list herein several AI LegalTech related products.

The information about them is being shown herein via whatever they have publicly stated via their websites.

This means that you should take whatever they've stated with a grain of salt.

If you are interested in any of these, it would be prudent to do appropriate follow-up research in order to try and ascertain and validate any claims being made.

This is not an exhaustive list of companies and only a sampling of some. No endorsement about these firms is implied and nor intended.

Blue J Legal

Source: https://www.bluejlegal.com/

Product Name: Tax Foresight

Tagline: "Instincts are good. Foresight is better. Blue J's AI-powered platform accurately predicts court outcomes and enables you to find relevant cases faster than ever before."

Stated Claims:

- "Support your position with predictions that are 90% accurate
- Access insights from the entire body of case law, updated weekly
- Slash research time and increase your workload capacity
- Standardize how issues are handled throughout your organization
- Train juniors to identify factors that matter
- Raise the benchmark of research quality"

Company Background:

"Blue J Legal uses machine learning and artificial intelligence to make the law more transparent and accessible. The company's technology saves researchers hours of time and offers confident answers in challenging circumstances."

"Our genesis began in 2014 with IBM's Watson Challenge at the University of Toronto. Benjamin Alarie, an associate dean at the time, was approached to help judge the competition, a contest between students and startups to create commercial implementations for the technology company's super-computer AI.

Benjamin was intrigued by the possibilities of applying AI to tax law. By 2015, our first prototype was built. Within a year, Blue J Legal began selling Tax Foresight, its first product, commercially. Since then, the company has expanded its product offering to include Employment Foresight, and most recently, HR Foresight."

"Today, Blue J Legal has established itself as a market leader in producing legal technology powered by machine learning and artificial intelligence. Based in the heart of downtown Toronto, we are a cutting edge startup with a diverse and high-performing team. Our team includes former Bay Street lawyers from McCarthy Tétrault, Torys, and Gowling WLG, law professors from the University of Toronto, management consultants, engineers, and data scientists."

Casetext Inc.

Source: https://casetext.com/

Product Name: Compose and CARA A.I.

Tagline: "Litigation automation is finally here. Introducing Compose, a revolutionary new brief automation tool from the makers of Casetext."

Stated Claims:

- "Better results in less time.
- Leverage advanced research tools to find on-point authorities in your first search — not your tenth.
- Use your favorite search techniques or advanced A.I. search to get the right results, fast.
- Based on what it knows about your matter, CARA A.I. searches Casetext's database for the most relevant results.
- Upload a document from your case to CARA A.I. to find authorities with the same legal issues, facts, and jurisdiction — no need to construct a complex search query.
- Drag and drop opposing counsel's brief into CARA A.I. to see the authorities they didn't find — or intentionally left out.
- Run your draft brief through CARA A.I. to be sure you've found all the best support for your arguments, and that it's still good law."

Company Background:

"At Casetext we believe that all attorneys should have access to quality legal research. So, we built an award-winning legal research platform that makes research faster and more accurate using advanced artificial intelligence. Then we priced our service so every attorney can afford it."

"Casetext is headquartered in San Francisco, with offices in New York, Austin, Washington D.C., and Kansas City."

eBREVIA

Source: https://ebrevia.com/

Product Name: eBrevia

Tagline: "Contract Review and Data Extraction powered by AI"

Stated Claims:

- "At least 10% more accurate than manual review alone
- 30-90% faster than manual review alone
- Seamlessly upload and review documents in an easy-to-use interface, with extensive workflow features.
- Deliver actionable intelligence with summaries exported directly to Word, Excel or your database or contract management system.
- Train the software to extract custom data in multiple languages"

Company Background:

"eBrevia is now a subsidiary of Donnelley Financial Solutions (DFIN), a leading global risk and compliance solutions company. eBrevia's cutting-edge contract analytics is a key part of DFIN's robust ecosystem that provides domain expertise, enterprise software and data analytics in every stage of business and investment lifecycles."

Everlaw

Source: https://www.everlaw.com/

Product Name: Everlaw Discover, Reveal, Act

Tagline: "Promoting justice by illuminating truth. Everlaw is a cloud-native ediscovery solution that unlocks the collaborative power of teams to investigate issues more thoroughly, uncover truth more quickly, and present their findings more clearly."

Stated Claims:

- "Machine Learning. Expedite and prioritize review by surfacing relevant documents more easily and quickly than ever. Leverage supervised and unsupervised machine learning in every case with predictive coding and document clustering.

- Predictive Coding. Improve review efficiency and accuracy by prioritizing review on documents with predicted likelihood of being relevant, by teaching the system with assigned ratings, codes and attributes.
- Advanced Analytics. Review and understand all documents continuously in the Everlaw platform, whether they be foreign language documents, media files, or emails. Explore data at a glance without the need to review individual documents or conduct a predetermined search."

Company Background:

"March 11, 2020. Everlaw, an Oakland, Calif.-based electronic discovery and litigation service, completed a $62 million Series C. CapitalG and Menlo Ventures led the investment, which included participation from Andreessen Horowitz and K9 Ventures. Jesse Wedler, partner at CapitalG, will join the board."

LawGeex

Source: https://www.lawgeex.com/

Product Name:

Tagline: "LawGeex is empowering lawyers to be the lawstars they were always meant to be. See how LawGeex automates your contract review so you can focus on your business."

Stated Claims:

- "We combine AI with human expertise to automatically detect missing clauses, or commonly-overlooked risks.
- Remove all unnecessary roadblocks from the process so your business flows faster and more smoothly.
- Integrating into your existing workflow is easy – no complicated installation or expensive hardware needed.
- Free your legal team to work more efficiently, make stronger deals, and build a better business.

- Standardizing the contract review process gives you smoother hand-offs, fewer glitches, and better communication throughout your organization."

Company Background:

"As the pioneers of Contract Review Automation, LawGeex enables your legal team to focus on more impactful legal work. With offices in Tel Aviv and New York City, LawGeex is trusted by some of the world's largest companies, like eBay, White & Case, and Office Depot."

Leverton

Source: https://leverton.ai/

Product Name: Leverton

Tagline: "Data-driven decisions faster with Leverton Artificial Intelligence. Leverton is a patented, award-winning AI-powered data extraction and contract analytics platform for corporate and legal documents."

Stated Claims:

- "Leverton Artificial Intelligence (AI) extracts key data from your documents and links each extracted data point to the source information. We then validate all extracted data via a two-step quality check and control process.
- Access and analyze structured data in a variety of dashboards from pivot tables to calendars of critical dates.
- Leverton reduces manual abstraction costs by up to 50% and identifies opportunities for cost savings and increased revenue that go unnoticed
- Leverton speeds up mundane data extraction processes by 50% to 75%, enabling employees to spend more time doing more strategic, higher-value tasks."

Company Background:

"We are the AI technology pioneer in data extraction and contract analytics for corporate and legal documents."

"Leverton was founded in 2012 by a group of scientists looking to push the boundaries of artificial intelligence for semantic analysis. Since then, the Company has transformed from a laboratory experiment to a robust, AI-powered data extraction and contract analytics platform. From the very beginning, we were founded on the principles of turning unstructured content into structured data, regardless of the look and feel of the source information. We use a set of proprietary and patented machine and deep learning algorithms, our own optical character recognition ("OCR") engine, pattern recognition, natural language processing, and grammatical syntax structure detection to deliver a state-of-the-art experience for our customers.

Leverton has transformed into a Software-as-a-Service (SaaS) that anyone can use, whether you are a small business or a Fortune 500 company. Our humble beginnings led us to service many different industries and use cases including real estate, finance, insurance, healthcare, shipping, telecommunications, and many more. In 2019, Leverton was acquired by MRI Software, LLC, a global leader in real estate software solutions with offices throughout North America, Europe, Asia, Australia, and Africa. As part of the MRI family, we are continuing our mission to help businesses worldwide make smarter decisions using better data."

Conclusion

Please do take a look at the resources mentioned in this chapter.

You'll be glad that you did.

Dr. Lance B. Eliot

CHAPTER 12
IT'S A WRAP,
UNTIL TOMORROW

CHAPTER 12

IT'S A WRAP,

UNTIL TOMORROW

I hope that the chapters have gotten you up-to-speed on AI and its application to legal activities, along with providing an understanding of LegalTech and where it is headed, including the exciting and vital role that AI will be in improving and enhancing LegalTech.

My aim was to provide a balance about what today's AI can do, distinguishing it from the vision or dreams of what AI might someday be able to do.

And, to make clear, there isn't a robo-lawyer being cooked-up in AI research labs today that is suddenly going to appear on the scene.

If you were shaking in your boots about that possibility, you've got time before that's going to occur.

Nonetheless, despite being quite afar from an autonomous AI robot lawyer, there are valuable aspects that even today's AI can do to aid human lawyers and human-run law practices.

Let's do a quick recap of key salient points covered in the chapters, though please don't be one of those readers that looks only at the last chapter and doesn't bother to read the rest of the book (you know who you are!).

In terms of those that are interested in AI and the law, I usually depict AI and the law as consisting of two primary areas of focus:

- AI as applied to the law

- Law as applied to AI

The focus of this book is about AI as applied to the law, meaning that there are fruitful ways that AI can be used to aid in the undertaking of legal activities.

Outside the scope of this particular book is the other topic, namely law as applied to AI, which usually consists of ascertaining how the law might need to be changed or reconsidered in light of what AI might be able to accomplish (a kind of governance notion about AI and how our laws might adjust to accommodate artificially "thinking" machines).

As an aside, I'm composing a book on that fascinating topic and look forward to sharing my thoughts soon about the rather meaty and at times controversial aspects involved.

Okay, back to the primary focus of AI applied to the law.

For practitioners of the law, they face numerous ongoing pressures about how to best conduct their legal activities.

Those pressures are increasingly going to force lawyers and law practices to rethink how they do their work.

Probably, early retirement might be the only viable means to avoid having to cope with those pressures.

Here are some factors applying those inexorable pressures:

- LegalTech emergence

- Push for data-driven legal analytics

- Enterprise apps and suites for Law Offices

- Professional Conduct adherence

- Next-Gen tech-savvy lawyers

- Need for deep legal research and reasoning

- Global work-from-anywhere (networks)

- AI proclaimed shake-up's

Using technology to aid in performing legal activities is one means to make your work more efficient, effective, and otherwise has numerous benefits, assuming it is accomplished in sensible ways.

Law offices have been slow to embrace new technology.

A burgeoning arena is LegalTech, spurred by the ability to create and provide apps for legal activities and that can use the cloud, along with leveraging mobile devices, and otherwise tie into the grand convergence of ubiquitous computing (such as the rise of the Internet of Things or IoT).

LegalTech can be defined as digital technology that's oriented toward and applied to law firms, lawyers, and those in legal practices, for which the tech is intended to be instrumental toward and integral to the practice of the law and the performance of legal services.

The ABA some eight years ago added into the Model Rules of Professional Conduct an indication that lawyers have a duty to be competent in technology, and the latest version states this (in Rule 1.1, comment 8):

"To maintain the requisite knowledge and skill, a lawyer should keep abreast of changes in the law and its practice, including the benefits and risks associated with relevant technology, engage in continuing study and education and comply with all continuing legal education requirements to which the lawyer is subject."

That dovetails into the intent and spirit of ABA rule 1.1:

"A lawyer shall provide competent representation to a client. Competent representation requires the legal knowledge, skill, thoroughness, and preparation reasonably necessary for the representation."

If AI is going to become widely used in the effort of performing legal activities, and assuming it does well, there is a bona fide concern about the employment prospects of human lawyers, given that the AI might reduce the need for as many lawyers as otherwise might have been needed in a non-AI world.

In short, it could be that:

1. **Augment.** Lawyers will be augmented by AI, which is useful for lawyers, yet it could also mean that in the aggregate not as many lawyers are needed since a lawyer with an AI tool could potentially do the work of those other lawyers that might otherwise have been needed to meet workload demands.

2. **Replace.** Lawyers might be replaced by AI, doing so in specific and narrow areas, thus, reducing the volume of need for human lawyers (and though some speculate about the robo-lawyer replacing human lawyers altogether, that's just not in the cards for a long time to come.

All this talk in the media about the coming robo-lawyer tends to create confusion and at times overstate what AI can do and cannot do.

Thus, this raises two notable concerns:

1. AI that is touted as being able to replace human lawyers in their entirety will not be provable as being able to do so, raising the specter that the legal advice so given by the AI system is potentially suspect, brittle, or otherwise weaker than a human lawyer

2. AI that is touted as being able to replace human lawyers could be a boast or promise that misleads the public in a willingness to use such AI systems, not realizing the peril it entails (under the assumption that the AI is not able to do so).

It is important to understand what AI truly consists of.

AI is really two aspects at once:

1. Seeking to have machines artificially achieve human intelligence

2. Do #1 via the use of various technologies (umbrella of tech)

The primary subfields of AI consist of:

- Machine Learning (ML)

- Knowledge-Based Systems (KBS)

- Natural Language Processing (NLP)

- Computer Vision (CV)

- Robotics / Autonomy

- Common-Sense Reasoning

- Other Technologies

For law offices and lawyers, here are the various legal activities that they carry out:

- Case Management

- Contracts

- Courts/Trials

- Discovery

- Documents/Records

- IP

- Law Office/Practice

- Lawyer & Client Interaction

- Legal Assistants

- Legal Collaboration

- Legal Research

- Legal Workflow

- Legal Writing

- Professional Conduct

- Other

It is handy therefore to consider a matrix consisting of the AI Technologies as corresponding to each of the Legal Activities listed above.

Trying to put in place AI can be especially difficult if the underlying legal activity is not already aided by some form of digital tech, such as conventional LegalTech.

Generally, trying to add AI would require a two-step of first moving beyond manual methods of performing the task and getting it into a digital realm that is amenable to then using AI.

The existing marketplace is rather sparse in terms of AI solutions that work with LegalTech and the various legal activities.

That's "bad" due to the paucity of options currently available.

That's "good" because it means that the market is wide open and lots of untapped opportunities abound.

For those of you seeking to identify an opportunity and potentially get a startup going, there are two ways to potentially proceed:

1. Start with a Legal Activity in the list and then explore the AI side of things, or

2. Start with an AI tech and then explore the legal activity side of things

Conclusion

The thrill of being in AI is that each day produces yet another new advance related to AI tech.

This also means that you cannot just be sitting around and have your head in the sand since the AI that you thought you knew might be eclipsed by newer and better AI capabilities.

Now that you've come up with the learning curve on the topic of AI and LegalTech, please continue your progress.

The prior chapter and the Appendix of this book offer numerous ways that you can keep your interest going and stay on top of what's happening.

Note: *For supplemental materials depicting the aspects discussed in this chapter, refer to Appendix B, which contains various augmented diagrams, charts, and additional related facets of relevance.*

APPENDIX

APPENDIX A
TEACHING WITH THIS MATERIAL

The material in this book can be readily used either as a supplemental to other content for a class, or it can also be used as a core set of textbook material for a specialized class.

Classes where this material is most likely used include any classes at the college or university level that want to augment the class by offering thought provoking and educational essays about AI and/or Law.

In particular, here are some aspects for class use:

o   Computer Science. Classes studying AI, or possibly a CS social impacts class, etc.

o   Law. Law classes exploring technology and its adoption for legal uses.

o   Sociology. Sociology classes on the adoption and advancement of technology.

Specialized classes at the undergraduate and graduate level can also make use of this material.

For each chapter, consider whether you think the chapter provides material relevant to your course topic.

There is plenty of opportunity to get the students thinking about the topic and force them to decide whether they agree or disagree with the points offered and positions taken.

I would also encourage you to have the students do additional research beyond the chapter material presented (I provide next some suggested assignments they can do).

RESEARCH ASSIGNMENTS ON THESE TOPICS

Your students can find background material on these topics, doing so in various law journals and in technical publications (see the listings provided in Chapter 11).

Here are some suggestions of homework or projects that you could assign to students:

a) Assignment for foundational AI research topics: Research and prepare a paper and a presentation on a specific aspect of AI, Machine Learning, ANN, etc. The paper should cite at least 3 reputable sources. Compare and contrast to what has been stated in this book.

b) Assignment for Law topics: Research and prepare a paper covering Law aspects via at least 3 reputable sources and analyze the characterizations. Compare and contrast to what has been stated in this book.

c) Assignment for a Business topic: Research and prepare a paper and a presentation on businesses and advanced technology regarding LegalTech and/or AI. What is hot, and what is not? Cite at least 3 reputable sources. Compare and contrast to the depictions in this book.

d) Assignment to do a Startup: Have the students prepare a paper about how they might startup a business in this realm. They must submit a sound Business Plan for the startup. They could also be asked to present their Business Plan and so should also have a presentation deck to coincide with it.

You can certainly adjust the aforementioned assignments to fit to your particular needs and class structure.

You'll notice that I ask for 3 reputable cited sources for the paper writing based assignments.

I usually steer students toward "reputable" publications, since otherwise they will cite some oddball source that has no credentials other than that they happened to write something and post it onto the Internet.

You can define "reputable" in whatever way you prefer, for example some faculty think Wikipedia is not reputable while others believe it is reputable and allow students to cite it.

The reason that I usually ask for at least 3 citations is that if the student only does one or two citations, they usually settle on whatever they happened to find the fastest. By requiring three citations, it usually seems to force them to look around, explore, and end-up probably finding five or more, and then whittling it down to 3 that they will actually use.

I have not specified the length of their papers and leave that to you to tell the students what you prefer.

For each of those assignments, you could end-up with a short one to two pager or you could do a dissertation length paper. Base the length on whatever best fits for your class, and the credit amount of the assignment within the context of the other grading metrics you'll be using for the class.

I mention in the assignments that they are to do a paper and prepare a presentation. I usually try to get students to present their work. This is a good practice for what they will do in the business world. Most of the time, they will be required to prepare an analysis and present it. If you don't have the class time or inclination to have the students present, then you can of course cut out the aspect of them putting together a presentation.

GUIDE TO USING THE CHAPTERS

For each of the chapters, I provide next some various ways to use the chapter material.

You can assign the tasks as individual homework assignments, or the tasks can be used with team projects for the class. You can easily layout a series of assignments, such as indicating that the students are to do item "a" below for say Chapter 1, then "b" for the next chapter of the book, and so on.

a) What is the main point of the chapter and describe in your own words the significance of the topic,

b) Identify at least two aspects in the chapter that you agree with, and support your concurrence by providing at least one other outside researched item as support; make sure to explain your basis for disagreeing with the aspects,

c) Identify at least two aspects in the chapter that you disagree with, and support your disagreement by providing at least one other outside researched item as support; make sure to explain your basis for disagreeing with the aspects,

d) Find an aspect that was not covered in the chapter, doing so by conducting outside research, and then explain how that aspect ties into the chapter and what significance it brings to the topic,

e) Interview a specialist in industry about the topic of the chapter, collect from them their thoughts and opinions, and readdress the chapter by citing your source and how they compared and contrasted to the material,

f) Interview a relevant academic professor or researcher in a college or university about the topic of the chapter, collect from them their thoughts and opinions, and readdress the chapter by citing your source and how they compared and contrasted to the material,

g) Try to update a chapter by finding out the latest on the topic, and ascertain whether the issue or topic has now been solved or whether it is still being addressed, explain what you come up with.

The above are all ways in which you can get the students of your class involved in considering the material of a given chapter. You could mix things up by having one of those above assignments per each week, covering the chapters over the course of the semester or quarter.

APPENDIX B
SUPPLEMENTAL
FIGURES AND CHARTS

The following figures and charts augment the chapters, providing helpful visualizations covering the chapter contents

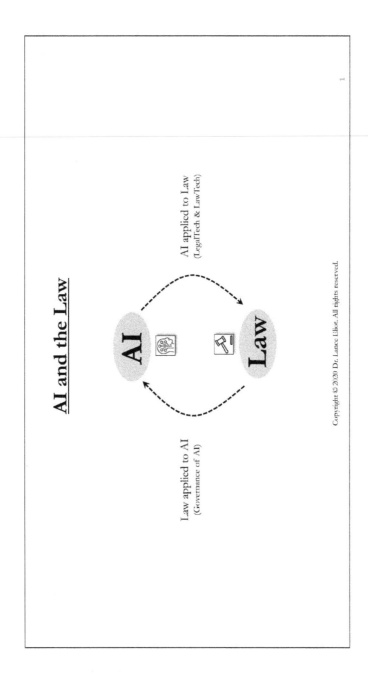

FIGURE 1

Dr. Lance B. Eliot

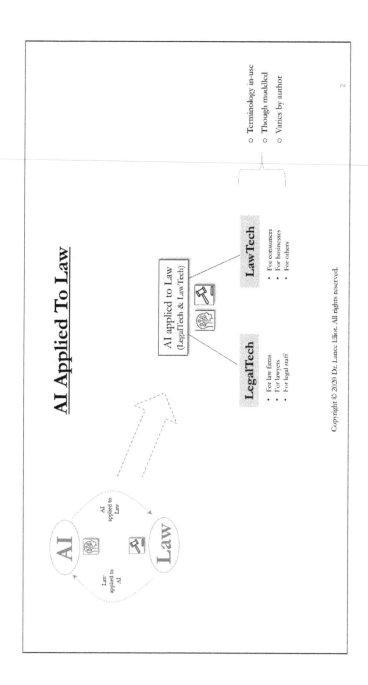

FIGURE 2

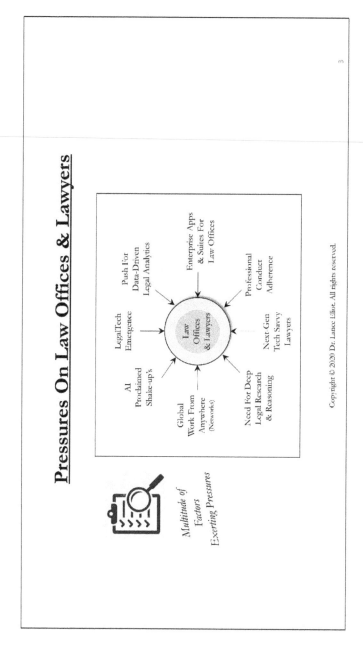

FIGURE 3

171

Dr. Lance B. Eliot

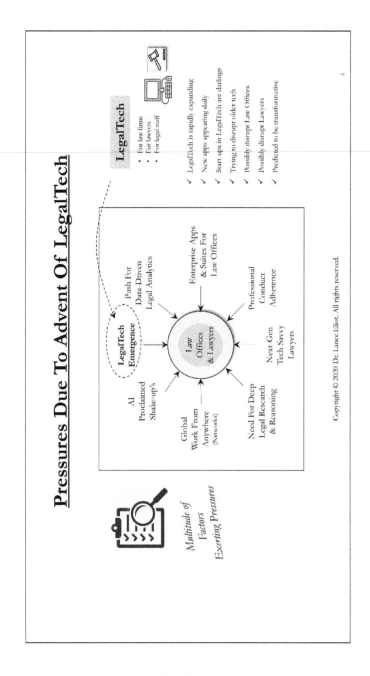

FIGURE 4

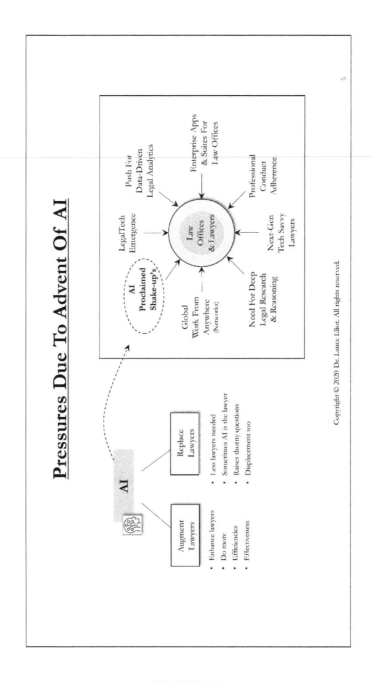

FIGURE 5

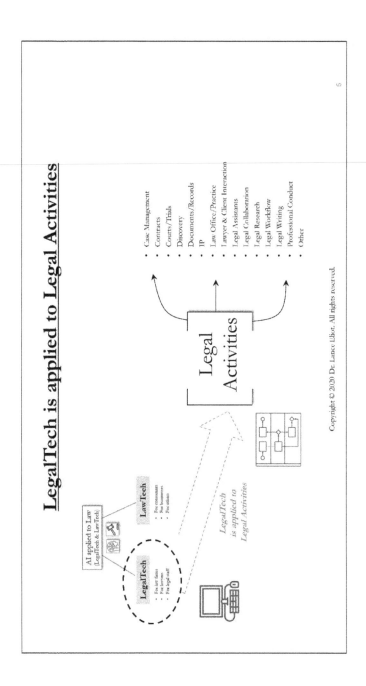

FIGURE 6

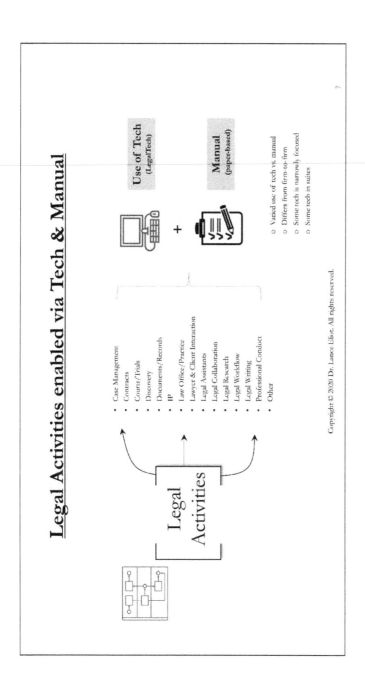

Legal Activities enabled via Tech & Manual

Legal Activities

- Case Management
- Contracts
- Courts/Trials
- Discovery
- Documents/Records
- IP
- Law Office/Practice
- Lawyer & Client Interaction
- Legal Assistants
- Legal Collaboration
- Legal Research
- Legal Workflow
- Legal Writing
- Professional Conduct
- Other

Use of Tech (LegalTech)

+

Manual (paper-based)

○ Varied use of tech vs. manual
○ Differs from firm-to-firm
○ Some tech is narrowly focused
○ Some tech in suites

FIGURE 7

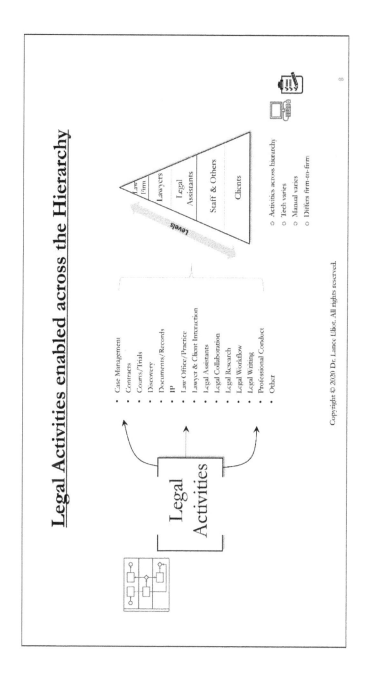

Legal Activities enabled across the Hierarchy

Legal Activities

- Case Management
- Contracts
- Courts/Trials
- Discovery
- Documents/Records
- IP
- Law Office/Practice
- Lawyer & Client Interaction
- Legal Assistants
- Legal Collaboration
- Legal Research
- Legal Workflow
- Legal Writing
- Professional Conduct
- Other

Levels

- Law Firm
- Lawyers
- Legal Assistants
- Staff & Others
- Clients

- Activities across hierarchy
- Tech varies
- Manual varies
- Differs firm-to-firm

8

FIGURE 8

181

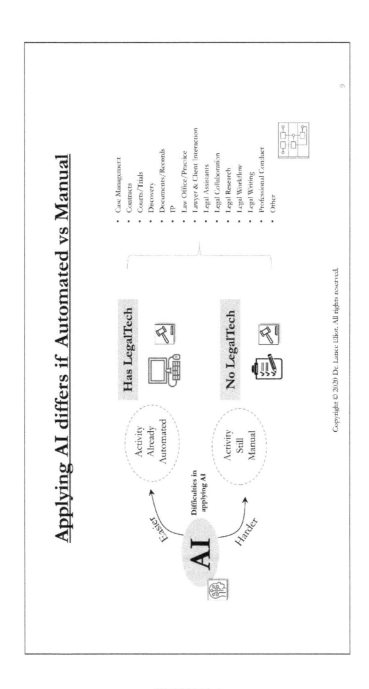

FIGURE 9

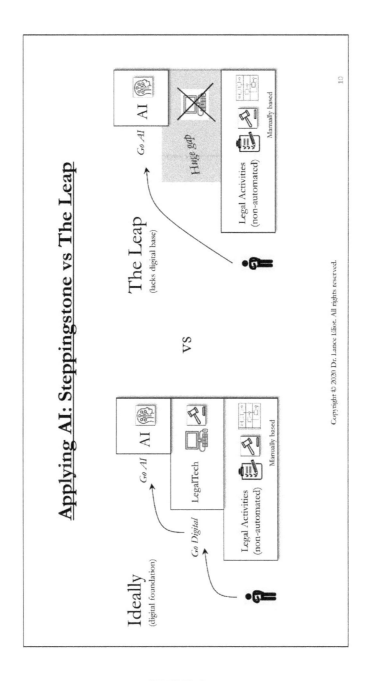

FIGURE 10

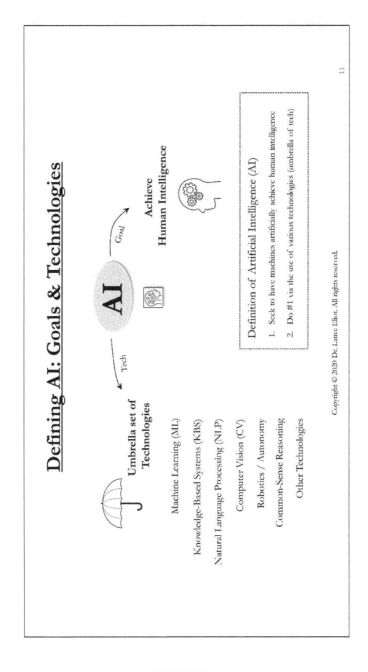

FIGURE 11

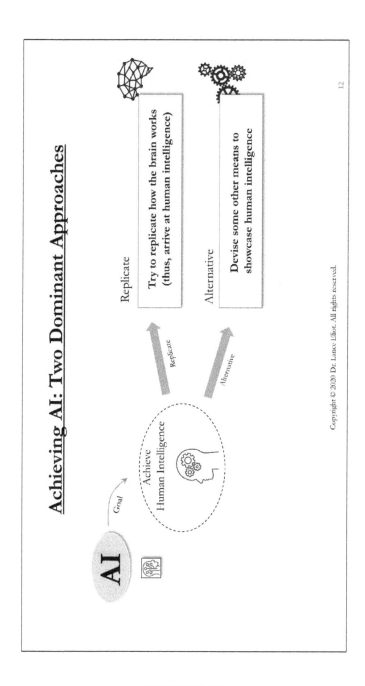

FIGURE 12

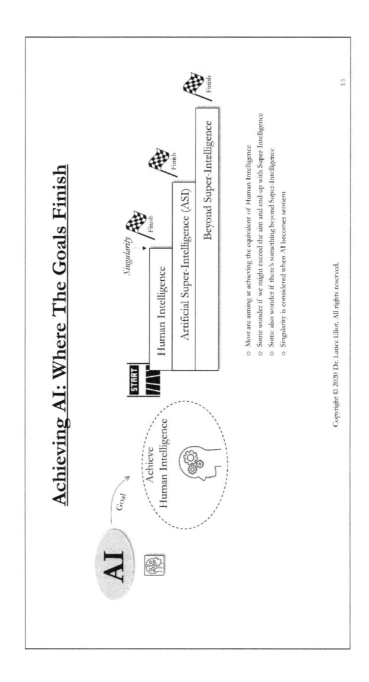

FIGURE 13

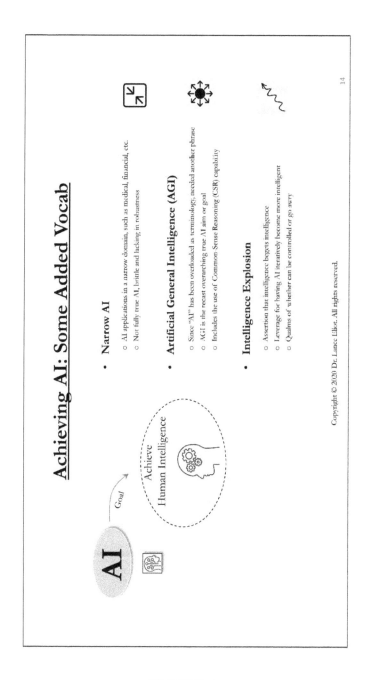

FIGURE 14

193

Dr. Lance B. Eliot

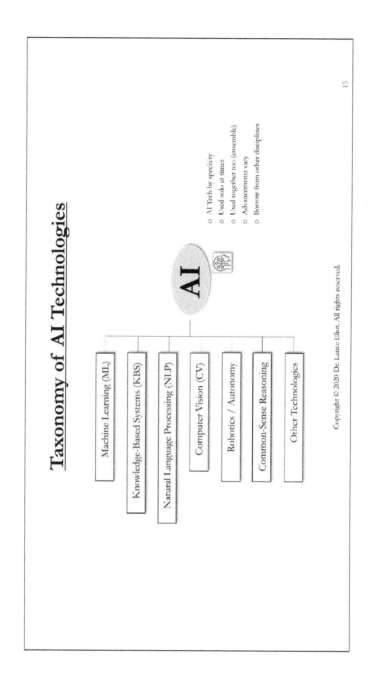

FIGURE 15

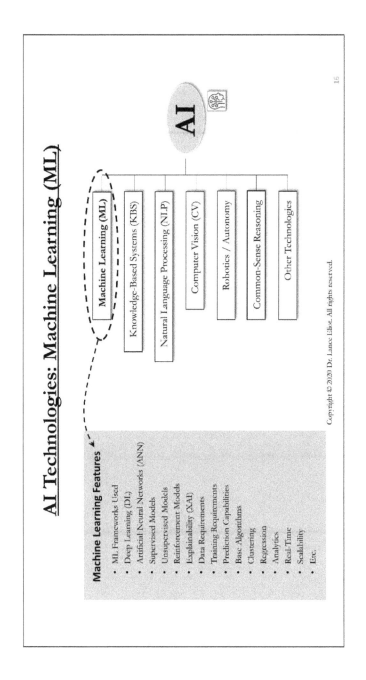

AI Technologies: Machine Learning (ML)

Machine Learning Features

- ML Frameworks Used
- Deep Learning (DL)
- Artificial Neural Networks (ANN)
- Supervised Models
- Unsupervised Models
- Reinforcement Models
- Explainability (XAI)
- Data Requirements
- Training Requirements
- Prediction Capabilities
- Basic Algorithms
- Clustering
- Regression
- Analytics
- Real-Time
- Scalability
- Etc.

Machine Learning (ML)

Knowledge-Based Systems (KBS)

Natural Language Processing (NLP)

Computer Vision (CV)

Robotics / Autonomy

Common-Sense Reasoning

Other Technologies

AI

FIGURE 16

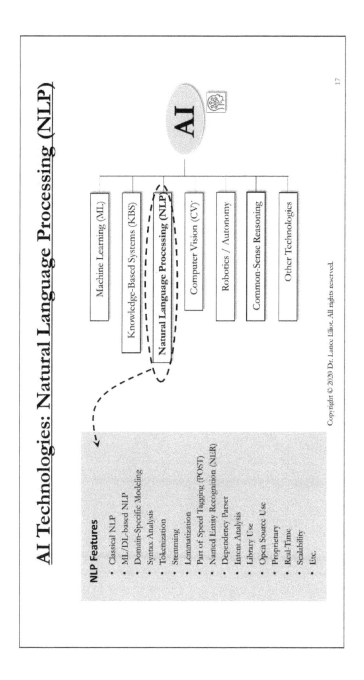

FIGURE 17

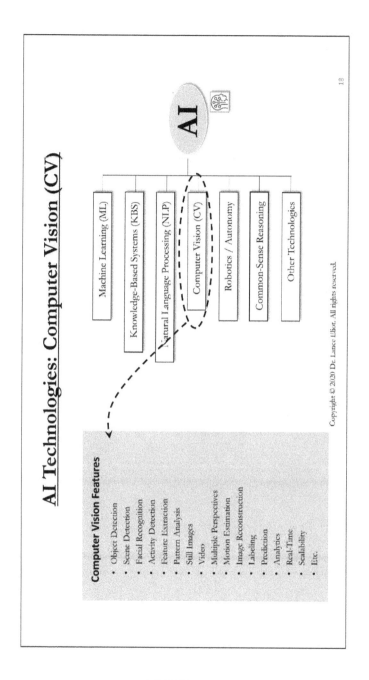

FIGURE 18

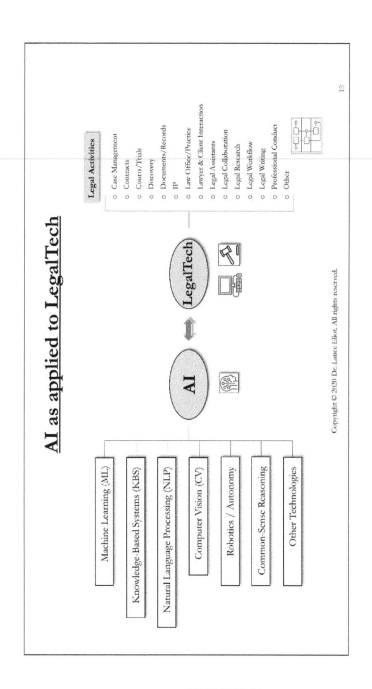

FIGURE 19

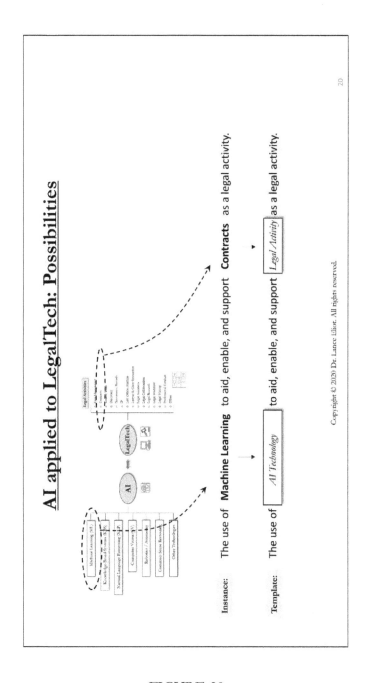

FIGURE 20

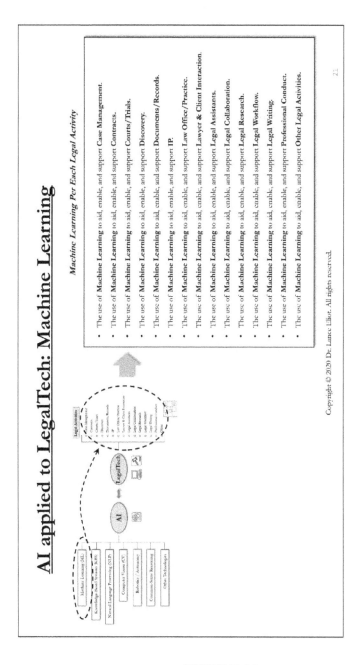

FIGURE 21

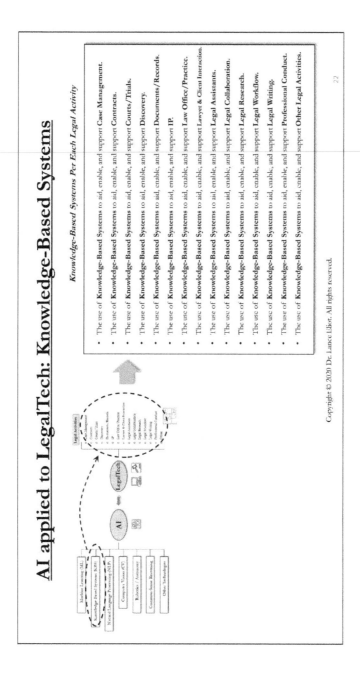

FIGURE 22

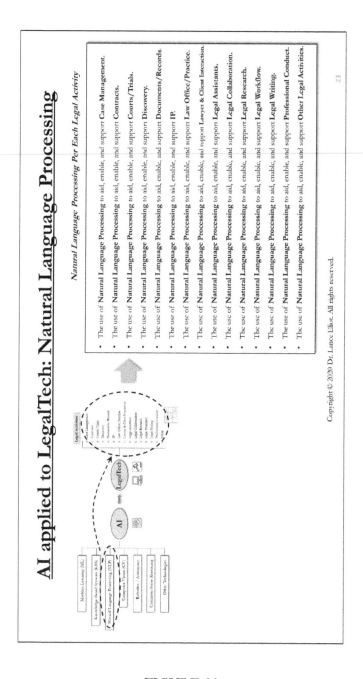

AI applied to LegalTech: Natural Language Processing

Natural Language Processing Per Each Legal Activity

- The use of **Natural Language Processing** to aid, enable, and support **Case Management.**
- The use of **Natural Language Processing** to aid, enable, and support **Contracts.**
- The use of **Natural Language Processing** to aid, enable, and support **Courts/Trials.**
- The use of **Natural Language Processing** to aid, enable, and support **Discovery.**
- The use of **Natural Language Processing** to aid, enable, and support **Documents/Records.**
- The use of **Natural Language Processing** to aid, enable, and support **IP.**
- The use of **Natural Language Processing** to aid, enable, and support **Law Office/Practice.**
- The use of **Natural Language Processing** to aid, enable, and support **Lawyer & Client Interaction.**
- The use of **Natural Language Processing** to aid, enable, and support **Legal Assistants.**
- The use of **Natural Language Processing** to aid, enable, and support **Legal Collaboration.**
- The use of **Natural Language Processing** to aid, enable, and support **Legal Research.**
- The use of **Natural Language Processing** to aid, enable, and support **Legal Workflow.**
- The use of **Natural Language Processing** to aid, enable, and support **Legal Writing.**
- The use of **Natural Language Processing** to aid, enable, and support **Professional Conduct.**
- The use of **Natural Language Processing** to aid, enable, and support **Other Legal Activities.**

FIGURE 23

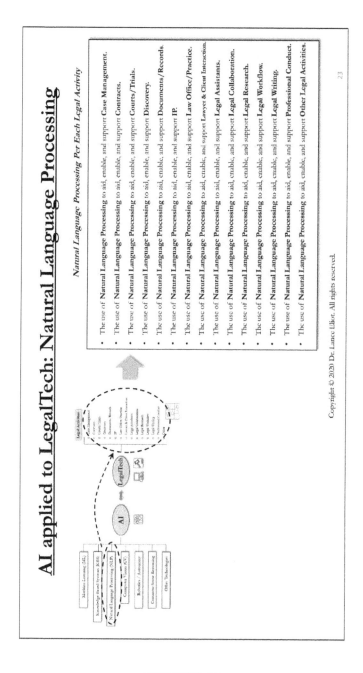

FIGURE 23

211

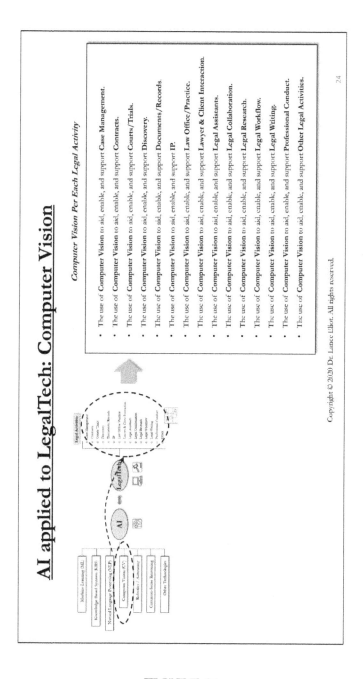

FIGURE 24

213

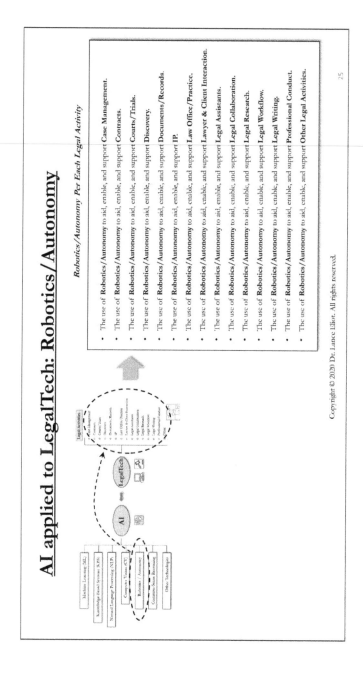

AI applied to LegalTech: Robotics/Autonomy

Robotics/Autonomy Per Each Legal Activity

- The use of **Robotics/Autonomy** to aid, enable, and support **Case Management.**
- The use of **Robotics/Autonomy** to aid, enable, and support **Contracts.**
- The use of **Robotics/Autonomy** to aid, enable, and support **Courts/Trials.**
- The use of **Robotics/Autonomy** to aid, enable, and support **Discovery.**
- The use of **Robotics/Autonomy** to aid, enable, and support **Documents/Records.**
- The use of **Robotics/Autonomy** to aid, enable, and support **IP.**
- The use of **Robotics/Autonomy** to aid, enable, and support **Law Office/Practice.**
- The use of **Robotics/Autonomy** to aid, enable, and support **Lawyer & Client Interaction.**
- The use of **Robotics/Autonomy** to aid, enable, and support **Legal Assistants.**
- The use of **Robotics/Autonomy** to aid, enable, and support **Legal Collaboration.**
- The use of **Robotics/Autonomy** to aid, enable, and support **Legal Research.**
- The use of **Robotics/Autonomy** to aid, enable, and support **Legal Workflow.**
- The use of **Robotics/Autonomy** to aid, enable, and support **Legal Writing.**
- The use of **Robotics/Autonomy** to aid, enable, and support **Professional Conduct.**
- The use of **Robotics/Autonomy** to aid, enable, and support **Other Legal Activities.**

FIGURE 25

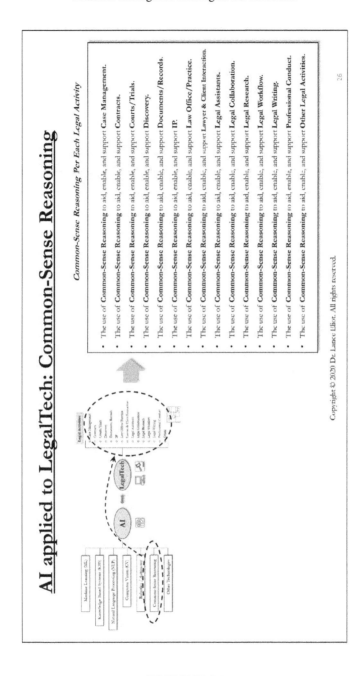

FIGURE 26

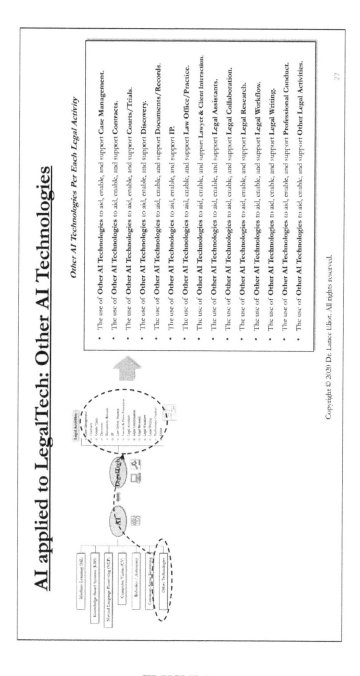

FIGURE 27

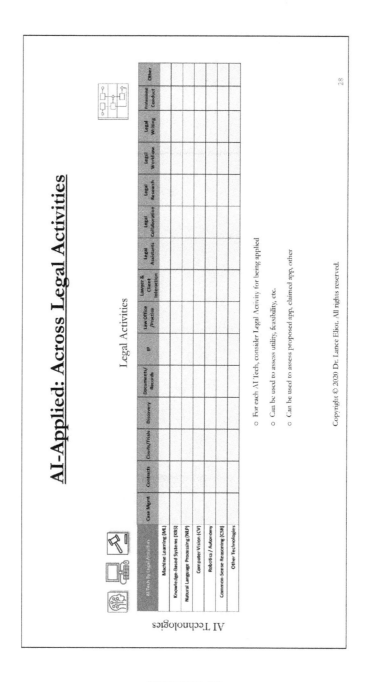

FIGURE 28

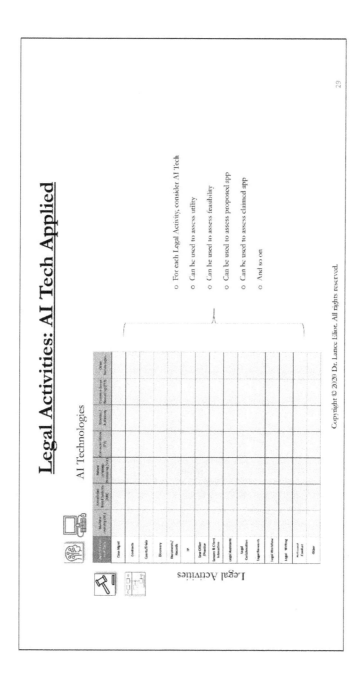

FIGURE 29

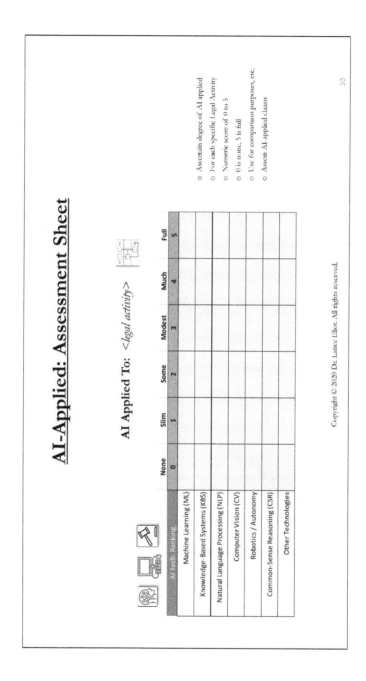

FIGURE 30

225

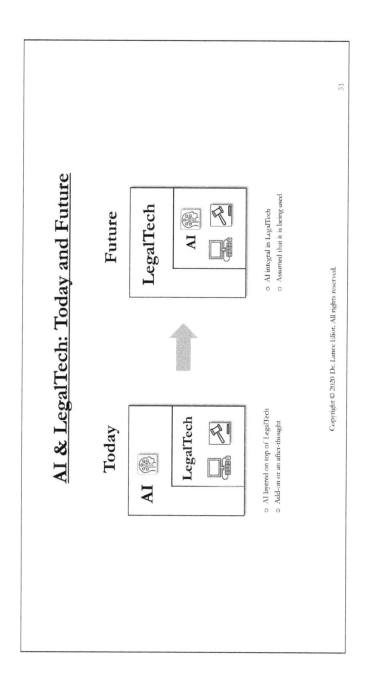

FIGURE 31

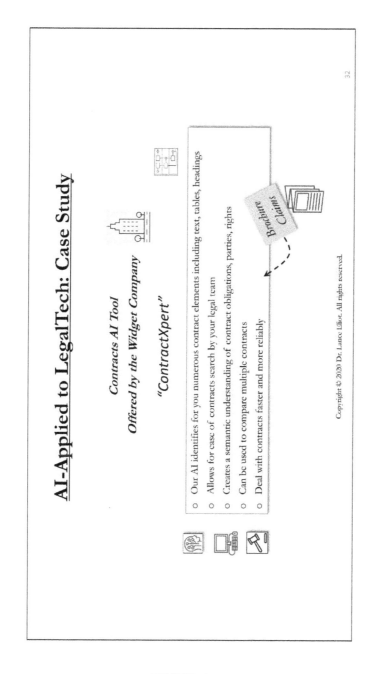

FIGURE 32

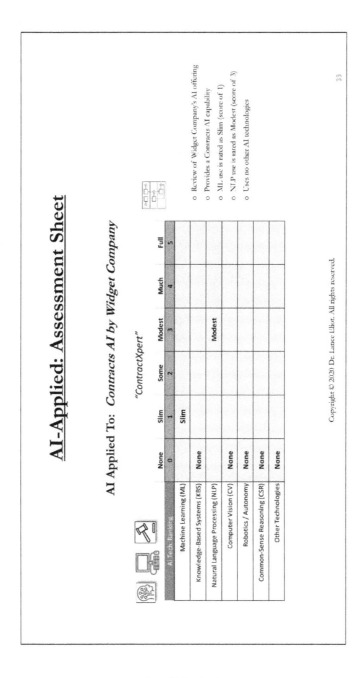

FIGURE 33

231

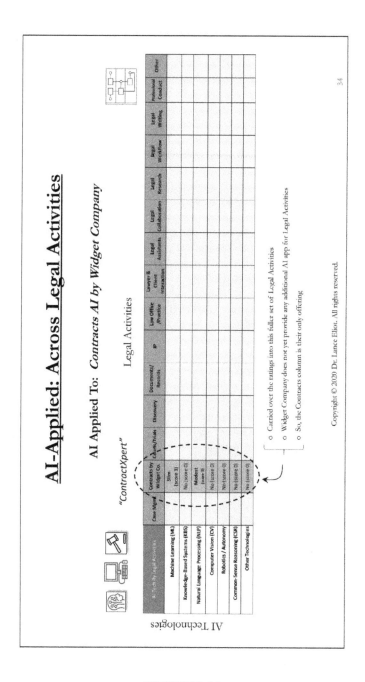

FIGURE 34

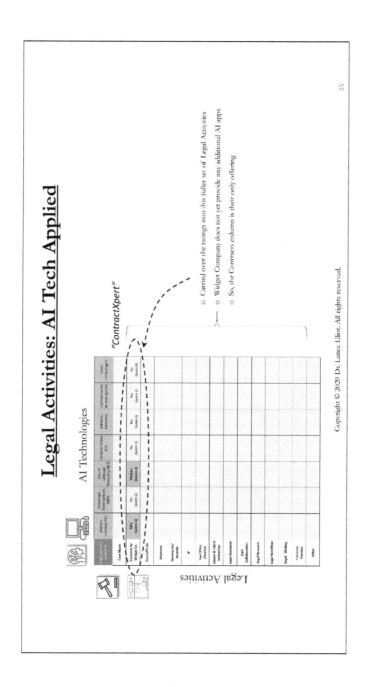

FIGURE 35

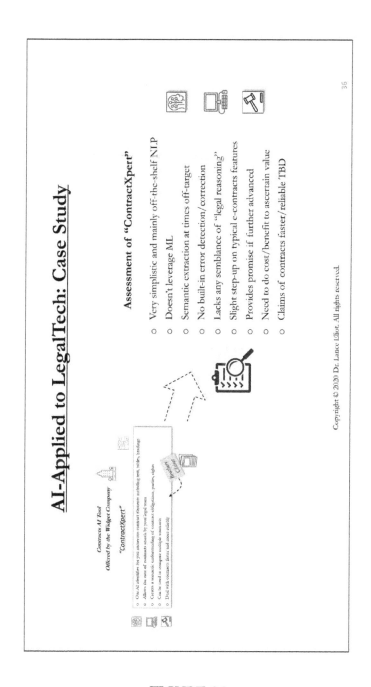

FIGURE 36

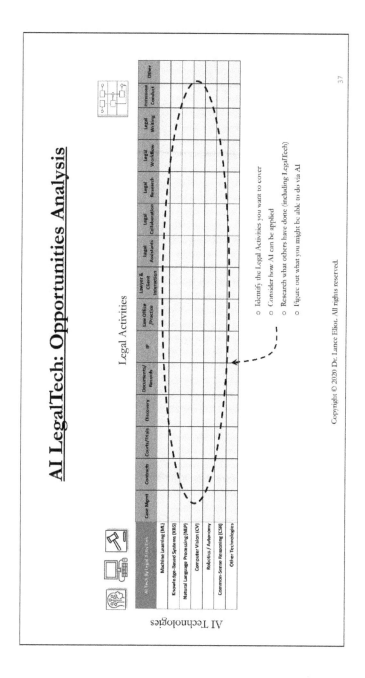

AI LegalTech: Opportunities Analysis

o Identify the Legal Activities you want to cover
o Consider how AI can be applied
o Research what others have done (including LegalTech)
o Figure out what you might be able to do via AI

FIGURE 37

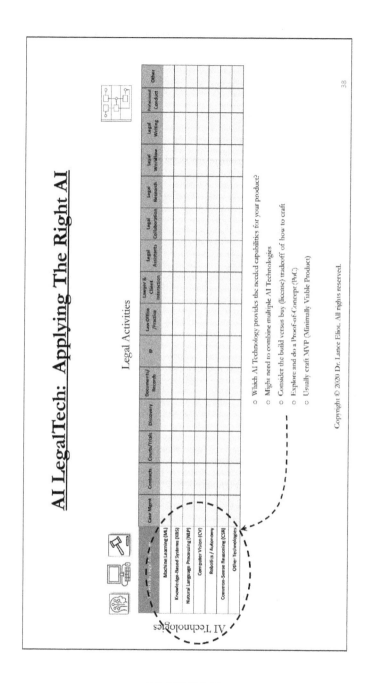

FIGURE 38

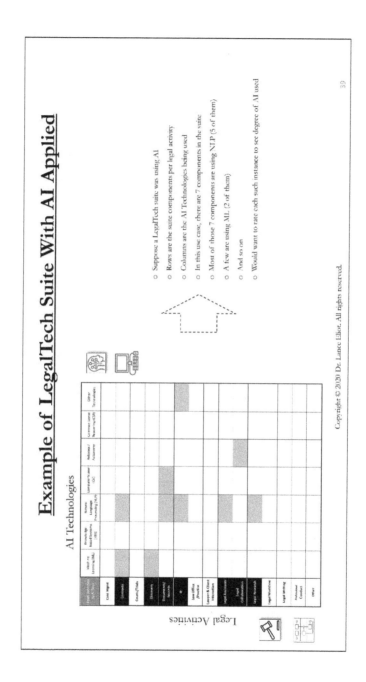

Example of LegalTech Suite With AI Applied

- Suppose a LegalTech suite was using AI
- **Rows** are the suite components per legal activity
- Columns are the AI Technologies being used
- In this use case, there are 7 components in the suite
- Most of those 7 components are using NLP (5 of them)
- A few are using ML (2 of them)
- And so on
- Would want to rate each such instance to see degree of AI used

FIGURE 39

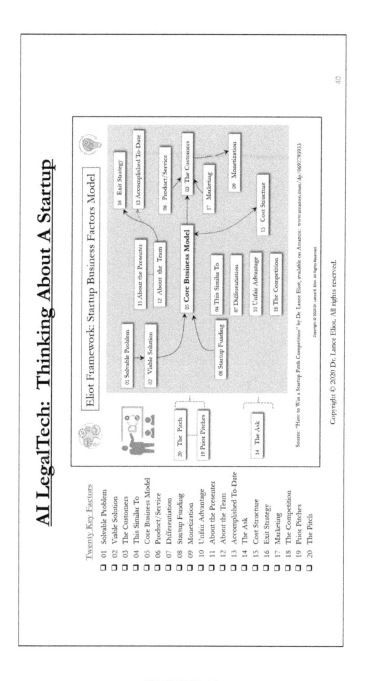

FIGURE 40

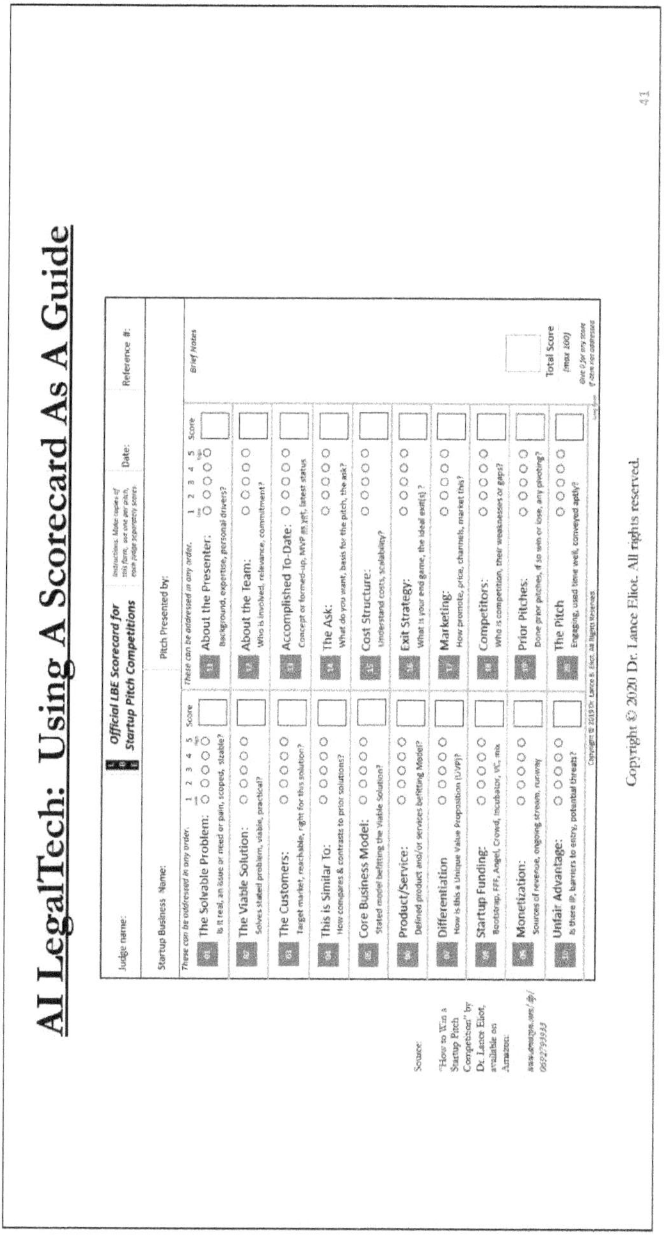

FIGURE 41

ABOUT THE AUTHOR

Dr. Lance B. Eliot, PhD, MBA is a globally recognized AI expert and thought leader, an experienced executive and leader, a successful serial entrepreneur, and a noted scholar on AI, including that his Forbes and AI Trends columns have amassed over 2.5+ million views, his books on AI are frequently ranked in the Top 10 of all-time AI books, his journal articles are widely cited, and he has developed and fielded dozens of AI systems.

He currently serves as the CEO of Techbruim, Inc. and has over twenty years of industry experience including serving as a corporate officer in billion-dollar sized firms and was a partner in a major consulting firm. He is also a successful entrepreneur having founded, ran, and sold several high-tech related businesses.

Dr. Eliot previously hosted the popular radio show *Technotrends* that was also available on American Airlines flights via their in-flight audio program, he has made appearances on CNN, has been a frequent speaker at industry conferences, and his podcasts have been downloaded over 100,000 times.

A former professor at the University of Southern California (USC), he founded and led an innovative research lab on Artificial Intelligence. He also previously served on the faculty of the University of California Los Angeles (UCLA), and was a visiting professor at other major universities. He was elected to the International Board of the Society for Information Management (SIM), a prestigious association of over 3,000 high-tech executives worldwide.

He has performed extensive community service, including serving as Senior Science Adviser to the Vice Chair of the Congressional Committee on Science & Technology. He has served on the Board of the OC Science & Engineering Fair (OCSEF), where he is also has been a Grand Sweepstakes judge, and likewise served as a judge for the Intel International SEF (ISEF). He served as the Vice Chair of the Association for Computing Machinery (ACM) Chapter, a prestigious association of computer scientists. Dr. Eliot has been a shark tank judge for the USC Mark Stevens Center for Innovation on start-up pitch competitions and served as a mentor for several incubators and accelerators in Silicon Valley and Silicon Beach.

Dr. Eliot holds a PhD from USC, MBA, and Bachelor's in Computer Science, and earned the CDP, CCP, CSP, CDE, and CISA certifications.

ADDENDUM

Artificial Intelligence And LegalTech Essentials

Advanced Series On

Artificial Intelligence (AI) and Law

By

Dr. Lance B. Eliot, MBA, PhD

———

For special orders of this book, contact:

LBE Press Publishing

Email: LBE.Press.Publishing@gmail.com

www.ingramcontent.com/pod-product-compliance
Lightning Source LLC
Chambersburg PA
CBHW051047050326
40690CB00006B/634